Overindulged Children:

A Parent's Guide to Mentoring

REVISED

Dr. James A. Fogarty

Licensed Clinical Psychologist
Certified School Psychologist

Liberty Publishing Group
Egg Harbor • Frederick • Raleigh

This publication is designed to provide accurate and
authoritative information in regard to the subject matter covered.
It is sold with the understanding that the publisher is not engaged
in rendering legal, accounting or other professional service.
From a Declaration of Principles jointly adopted by a Committee
of the American Bar Association and a Committee of Publishers.

Publisher's Cataloging-in-Publication Data

Fogarty, James A..
Overindulged Children: A parent's guide to
mentoring./ James A. Fogarty.
p. cm.

ISBN 1-893095-41-X
1. Parenting   2. Interpersonal communication
I. Title

Library of Congress Control Number: 2005924360

10 9 8 7 6 5 4 3 2 1

"Put your pocketbook away! Love 'em, don't overindulge 'em!

(Jim Fogarty)

Dedication

I dedicate this book to my Dad and my Irish uncles—the greatest mentors in the world. Each was filled with personality and a great smile:

- Adrian Fogarty – My blue-eyed and red-headed dad and all-purpose mentor.
- Myron Fogarty – The horse lover, who I spent many Saturdays. He taught me to mentor children.
- Frank Fogarty – The mechanic who could fix anything. He taught me to mentor with humor.
- Hank Fogarty – The uncle with the greatest smile. He taught me to mentor with a smile.
- Lester Fogarty – The colorful storyteller. He taught me to mentor with metaphor.
- Emmett Fogarty – The hard worker, who I enjoyed working with side by side. He was a great mentor for hard and persistent work.
- Justin Fogarty – Died of tuberculosis before I was born.
- Ray Fogarty – Died during World War II in France.
- Justin and Ray – Taught me there is a limit to our mentoring and our impact.

Acknowledgements

Family is the greatest concept ever created. Millions of families work throughout each day to love, talk, strive, survive, and bond. Families come in many forms and fashions. I would like to thank the families that have allowed me to enter their lives. I learned from each family and I appreciate the education.

She organizes, helps everyone, volunteers, sells classic antiques, perpetually smiles and gets me to do projects I never imagined I could do. She is my wife, Cyndy. Because of her I have been on three-story scaffolds, refurbished houses, built furniture, turned a factory into an antique shop, jumped off a cliff, installed a tin ceiling, written books, and lectured nationally. She shows me a picture of a piece of furniture, smiles and says, "You can do that!" Our favorite songs are "Hooked on a Feeling"—the Ooga Cuga version—and "Your Wildest Dreams." Married for 30 years—and it has been a wild dream to be hooked on this feeling!

The best feeling in the world is watching the birth of your children. The next best feeling is watching them become neat adults. They did it and I am very proud of Jason and Shawn. And Jason's new wife Theresa! And the newest Fogarty, their baby! He or she is still in production!

As always, thank you God.

Table of Contents

~ Introduction ~

Have you ever wondered why your children seem distant, in spite of your best efforts to make your children happy? Are you curious about why your children seem bored, detached, and disillusioned, even though they have every entertainment available? Have you been sold on the idea that children are the greatest priority in your family, a greater priority than your marriage? Have you felt pressure to buy the "right toy" for Christmas, with the belief that your child's Christmas would be ruined without it? Did you know that most homes have three or more televisions, with families detaching as family members isolate to watch their favorite programs? Overindulgence creates distance, and distance creates unhappy families.

Today is a time of prosperity, but there are more children flunking classes, truant, getting arrested, taking guns to school, dropping out of high school, and quitting jobs without giving notice than ever before. How have caring parents lost their influence with their children?

Many well-intended parents instill a false self-esteem within their children by overindulging them under the guise of "child-centered" families. The hope of many caring and well-intended parents is that their children will appreciate their "child-centered" parenting with greater appreciation, love, and bonding. Instead, these children have more conduct problems, opposition, indifference, detachment, and feelings of entitlement. They demand more luxuries and freedoms from their parents than ever before.

This book reveals the overindulgent beliefs that drive caring parents into overindulging their children. These overindulgent beliefs push well-intended parents to offer false love that instills within their children inflated and unrealistic views of themselves. You want to be close to your children. This book offers you the qualities of the mentoring parent, which gives empowered hope. Of course, empowered hope is the first step toward positive change.

I once read a bumper sticker that said, "Now that I have given up all hope, I feel better." Nothing could be further from the truth! Hope is the wish for change. Taking action is the agent of change. This book tells you what actions to take to become mentoring parents, so you can have a close relationship with your children.

What Is In This Book?

Chapter 1, "How Parents Overindulge Their Children," describes nine parenting styles that are overindulgent. One endearing quality of most overindulgent parents is that they truly love their children. These parents have special and unique qualities, but problems arise when they distort their special qualities. You will learn how caring parents can easily distort their special qualities and become overindulgent.

In Chapter 2, "What Overindulgence Parents Believe," you will explore the overindulgent beliefs many parents hope will gain their children's happiness. I also explain why these beliefs do not get you the closeness with your children that you desire and deserve.

Chapter 3, "The Qualities of the Mentoring Parent," teaches you the solution to stop overindulgent parenting. These parenting qualities are not theories; they are practical and usable parenting beliefs and skills designed to replace overindulgent parenting. You will like these skills! They work!

Chapter 4, "The Unsolved Mystery of Children's Misbehavior—Solved!" describes the motives behind your children's misbehavior. You will learn the reasons for children's back-talk, nagging, whining, button pushing, scapegoating, lying and other unacceptable behaviors. You will learn how overindulgence makes your children's behavior worse! You will also build your skills to mentor your children away from problem behaviors.

In Chapter 5, "The Toolbox for the Mentoring Parent," you will receive an array of parenting tools which, coupled with the personal qualities of the mentoring parent, will help you become the effective parent you want to be.

Let's get ready to change your basic beliefs about parenting and instill hope in your heart. Let's read!

~ CHAPTER 1 ~

How Parents Overindulge
Their Children

It is natural that parents want their children to be happy. I believe that children's happiness is a good parenting goal. But overindulgent parents restrict their parenting to making their children constantly happy. When parents limit their parenting role, problems ignite because children need more than happiness.

In fact, mentoring parents occasionally make their children feel bad. If you had mentoring parents, there are times they actually made you feel bad. They made you feel appropriate guilt and shame when you misbehaved. Then they taught you to make amends, so you would correct your misbehavior and relieve your guilt and shame. For example, Tommy intentionally broke his best friends' favorite toy. His mentoring parent said to Tommy, "This is one of those times when you should feel bad. So you need to make amends and here is what you need to do. Give your favorite toy to your friend." This instruction teaches Tommy to change his misbehavior, make amends with his friend and to release his guilt and shame. This instruction helps Tommy develop a conscience and stops him from becoming overindulged.

So what is overindulgence? Why does overindulgence happen? Do you have to be rich to overindulge your children? Is overindulgence only based on money and materialism? To begin to answer these questions, lets start with two definitions of overindulgence?

1. Parents, with wealth or *false wealth* (credit cards), replace mentoring their children with excessive materialism. Without mentoring, children do not develop critical life skills, such as:

    a. Conscience development, which teaches children when to make amends;
    b. Satisfying mutual relationship maintenance, which teaches children to maintain friendships;
    c. Self-reliance, which teaches children how to stand on their own two feet.

But there is another way to overindulge children that requires absolutely no money. Consider the second definition of overindulgence.

2. Parents, with no wealth or false wealth, can overindulge by giving their children too much permission too soon. Excessive permission puts children in situations they are not prepared to handle. This also creates a secondary danger—it puts children in the power-seat of their families, without the information, skills, or maturity needed to handle such a lofty position.

Notice that these two definitions suggest that overindulgent parents do not mentor their children. So, overindulgence becomes a replacement for mentoring. Mentoring occurs when parents guide and teach their children to manage the many parts of life. Overindulgent parents give materialism or permissions to their children, but they do not mentor to their children.

With these two definitions in mind, consider the three following examples. The first example is a wealthy family, the second example is a middle-income family, and the third example is a family with very little income.

The wealthy example:

This example will sound like a minor issue at first, but minor issues often reveal major issues, because they reflect long-standing patterns.

> *In a wealthy suburb of a large city, there is a beautiful high school surrounded by gorgeous and expensive homes. A student of this school complained to his parents that he was having trouble finding a parking place every morning, causing him to be late for school.*
>
> *What would you tell your teen if he or she could not find a parking place at school? You would probably offer a simple solution to this simple problem. For example, you might suggest leaving earlier or commuting with a friend. But his parents had a different plan. They bought a second home across the street from the high school—so their son could park his car in the driveway!*

This boy is not learning a basic life skill—how to manage a minor problem such as getting to school on time. If he is not learning the skills to manage this minor problem, what will happen when he needs to make a serious adjustment to a major issue? For example, what if he witnesses the violent death of one of his parents or friends in a car accident? This teen does not have the skills to get to school on time. How would he ever adjust to a difficult life issue?

Many children, in similar situations, do not learn to manage even the simplest problems of life.

The middle-income example:

When I present seminars in Nashville, my family goes because many of us play guitar. Nashville is guitar heaven and the center of guitar heaven is Gruhn's Guitar shop. As we were playing guitars, a mom walked in the guitar shop with her 8-year-old son. She bought him a $32,000 guitar.

I knew this was a middle-income family because the mom proudly told the salesman she emptied her retirement account to buy this guitar for her son. Since I was in Nashville, I thought this child might be a guitar prodigy. I asked the mom, "Can we hear him play?" She said, "Oh, no. He just started taking lessons."

This mom is stopping her son from learning a life-sustaining skill: that as he learns to progress, life will progress with him. Instead, he is learning that before he can progress, he needs the best—whether mom can afford it or not. Children need to experiment with many activities to uncover their skills and talents. A mentoring parent would buy him a $32.00 guitar. This boy, like most children, may play the guitar for two weeks and move on to other interests, which is natural for children. Her huge financial investment stops her ability to allow her son experiment with many activities.

The low-income example:

When I was a school psychologist, I worked for a very poor school district. A kindergarten student, whose parents enrolled him, was not coming to class. It was a week into the school year and he had not made a single appearance. I talked with his parents by phone. They seemed like nice folks and quite concerned for their child. However, two more weeks passed and he was still not attending school. With their permission, the school social worker and I went to their home for a home visit.

The family lived in a mobile home, with their grandmother and great-grandmother. As we all gathered in their living room to discuss the issue of their son's school attendance, this small boy was sitting on the floor, listening intently. During our discussion, he decided to demonstrate his power. He walked over to his dad, who was sitting in dad's favorite chair, and spryly said, "Dad, can I sit there?" His dad immediately popped up and let the boy take over the chair. The child sat there for five seconds.

Then he went over to his mother and, with the same demanding tone, said, "Mom, can I sit in your chair?" She immediately popped up from her chair and let him have her chair. He sat there for five seconds, as he looked at the social worker and me and smiled. Then he went to his grandmother, who was obese and very unhealthy. In fact, she was on oxygen. He looked her straight in the eyes and said, "Grandma, can I sit in your chair?" At that point, the social worker and I looked at each other with the same thought: "Is anyone going to stop this kid?" Grandmother leaned against the coffee table, strug-

*gling to get up from the couch while pulling her oxy-
gen, and let the child sit where she was sitting. He sat
there for five seconds. Then he headed for his great-
grandmother.*

Great-Grandmother, at 97 years old, was physically
frail but mentally sharp. She sat in a rocking chair because
it was easier for her to get up. The boy said to Great-Grandmother, "Can I sit in your chair?" She started rocking her
chair, propped herself up with her left hand and took a
swing at him with her right hand. She was frustrated
because she missed! But at least she made her point. Great-
Grandmother was not raised to get up for a 5-year-old, but she
was not in-charge of the family. The boy's parents were—or
were they? Who do you think was *really* in-charge?

Imagine this child at 15 years of age. You probably
don't have to—I'm sure you've experienced children like
this. They create problems in families, schools, communi-
ties and legal systems.

❧

Some professionals are losing their jobs due to
overindulged children.

*A teacher, with a very good work record, went above and
beyond. She assigned her high school students a term paper,
which was a major portion of their grade. Being resourceful,
she took the time to use the Internet, which has resources
teachers can use to determine if students plagiarize their
work. This took extra effort and time on the part of
this seasoned teacher. If her students plagiarized, they
did not really do the work and they cheated and lied.
To her dismay, this teacher discovered that 75% of
her students plagiarized! She appropriately failed the
cheaters.*

*Many of her students needed this credit to gradu-
ate and their parents sparked a revolution. Guess who
lost her job? This teacher gave her students what they
earned. She took the extra steps to insure her students' work was legitimate, and she lost her job. The
administration changed the students' grades and
allowed these cheaters to graduate. It is sad to see
excellent professionals actually lose their jobs due to
overindulgent families.*

I am a parent and a psychologist, trained to be an advocate for "child-centered" families. On the surface, the
phrase "child-centered" seems attractive and admirable. For
many years in my practice as a psychologist, I promoted a
"child-centered" approach to parenting. In fact, by using a
"child-centered" approach, I believed I had the answers to
every parenting problem. Befuddled, bewildered, and perplexed, I could not understand why these parenting principles
I worshiped failed the families I was trying to help.

Then I noticed a striking issue for families. Over the
last 23 years of counseling hundreds of families, I witnessed
a transfer of family power from parents to children. This
transfer of family power came under the guise of "child-
centered" parenting, with well-intended parents blending a
mix of advice from various parenting experts. Parents, who
deeply love their children, replaced mentoring their children
with overindulgence. In fact, the research suggests that this
transfer in power is the result of the soft structure that parents create for their children.

I believe many loving parents, driven by overindulgent
parenting beliefs, are losing influence with their children.
They are overindulging their children, but not bonding with
them. This is frightening to parents because the illusion of
overindulgence is seductive. Caring parents, lovingly give

to their children, hoping their children will reciprocate with love. These children are sweet, loving and beautiful children when they are in elementary school. Then they become demanding, angry and entitled – usually when they enter middle school!

Parents take many different avenues when overindulging their children. Let's take a look at these avenues and the impact they can have on children.

How Parents Overindulge Their Children

There are many different avenues for parents to overindulge their children. Most parents, who overindulge their children, have caring hearts and offer special qualities reflecting love for their children. Problems arise when parents distort these special qualities, and instead of giving children love and mentoring, they overindulge them.

Consider the following avenues for caring parents to overindulge their children.

Parents Who Give Too Much

The "giving" parent, as the name implies, is a giver, which is a wonderful quality. Some parents distort this special quality by giving their children too much materialism. "Giving" parents buy their children every brand-name toy and clothing on the market. No expense is spared! They love their children and to prove their love, they fill their children's bedrooms with televisions, computers, computer games, stereos, telephones, and more.

Parents, who give too much, expect their children to reciprocate with appreciation and love. This reciprocation often happens when children are young. As these overindulged children enter middle school and high school, they show little appreciation. Instead of love, these overindulged children feel resentment and entitlement.

There is a reason these children become a problem during middle school or high school years. As children develop they need skills to manage life. If mom and dad give them everything and do everything for them, their children do not learn life-management skills. So, they start to have problems as they gain more freedom, which usually occurs in middle school or high school.

Consider these examples of overindulgence:

During a counseling session with eight-year-old Ned, I asked him to describe his bedroom. Taking a deep breath, he said, "Well, I have a heated water bed and TV with a built-in VCR. It has a remote control and I am on cable with HBO and Cinemax. I have a private telephone line for my computer, and I'm on the Internet. I have Sega, Nintendo, Super Nintendo, and over 350 games. I have eight remote control cars and a remote control helicopter." Ned continued for ten more minutes. I checked my reaction, which was ENVY!

Elizabeth, a ten-year-old girl, refused to go to school unless she wore designer clothes! Her parents believed her desire to wear the best clothes money could buy reflected her positive self-esteem.

When Brad graduated from eighth grade, his parents rented a limousine to cruise Brad and his friends around town for several hours. Brad's parents said that this was the least they could do for him, as they were proud of their son. Brad was a bright child who was an underachiever, in the bottom 10% of his class—barely graduating.

~⚘~

Why would parents overindulge their children with expensive gifts? Here are several common reasons.

The Loving But Overindulgent Beliefs of "Giving" Parents:

1. By giving their children what they never had when they were children, some "giving" parents believe they are helping their children. These parents are actually attempting to fix their own childhood. In essence, these parents are overindulging themselves by overindulging their children.

    Although these "giving" parents strive for a loving relationship with their children, overindulged children rarely have a warm and loving feeling for their parents. When parents excessively give to their children, they are not teaching their children to manage life. Also, they are not bonding with their children. Instead, their children become over-dependent on their parents and often resent them. Instead of getting emotionally close, overindulgent children often separate from their parents—except when they want another toy, more money or a special activity.

This was the case with Ned, whose parents filled his room with expensive toys and goodies. Ned separated from his parents by isolating himself in his bedroom, which became his cocoon. He rarely left his cocoon, rejecting any involvement with his family. His parents' overindulgence of Ned created emotional distance, instead of the love his parents desired.

2. Some parents, who give too much, feel great competition with other parents who also overindulge their children. To keep up, they excessively give to their children with a "keep up with the Jones" parenting style. This "keep up with the Jones" attitude pushes parents into tremendous credit card debt (false wealth) for the sake of "giving" to their children. The sad reality is that all of this "giving" creates no real emotional bond between parents and children.

Brad's parents (who gave Brad the limousine ride they could not afford) did not really want to reward Brad for graduating at the bottom 10% of his class. There were many rewards within their budget that they could have given Brad, including rewards that did not involve exaggerated status symbols. In fact, they could have given him no reward.

Brad's parents never told their family and friends the truth about Brad's underachievement. In essence, they were rejecting the truth of Brad's lack of achievement, because Brad was a bright boy who chose to under-achieve! Brad was wasting his brain! Instead of confronting this problem, his parents taught Brad to put up a false, face-saving mask to save him from embarrassment.

Sometimes the truth is embarrassing—and it should be. For example, if you behave at work in a way that is embarrassing, your feeling of embarrassment teaches you lessons. When you attach good thinking to the uncomfortable emotion of embarrassment, you decide to never do embarrassing behavior at work again. So, the uncomfortable emotion of embarrassment, coupled with good thinking, creates self-guidance (I won't do that at work again). But Brad's parents erased his earned feelings of embarrassment by pretending he was successful in school. His parents also erased Brad's chance to gain good self-guidance.

3. Many "giving" parents are prone to guilt. This often happens with divorced parents. "Giving" parents, with guilt, try to release their guilt through excessive giving. Even at a tender age, children learn to take advantage of their parents' guilt. Children with guilt-ridden, overindulgent parents learn to guide their parents toward guilt-reducing purchases.

By using guilt trips, Elizabeth pressed her parents to believe that her friends would ridicule her for not wearing designer clothes to school. Her parents believed her and felt guilty. By buying her designer clothes, they thought they were helping her create good self-esteem. Instead, Elizabeth actually learned to use guilt-ridden manipulation to get what she wants from her parents.

You may be thinking that Elizabeth is right. Her friends will criticize her for not wearing designer clothes. This does happen! But, it is not a good reason for her parents to buy her designer clothes. Why? Because there are times in life when other people will have more than Elizabeth. So she needs to learn to adjust and feel okay about herself, no matter what she is wearing.

Ideas to Stop Giving Too Much to Your Children

- When your children do something wrong, allow them to feel the embarrassment and humiliation that naturally comes with their misbehavior. Always remember, there is good and bad embarrassment and humiliation. Brad, the bright child who underachieved, needed to feel embarrassed about his schoolwork. His mother was hiding Brad's failures from his grandparents by investing in a limousine. Brad needs to experience those embarrassing feelings. He needs to learn that to avoid embarrassment, he needs to change his behavior. He will never learn this lesson if his mother continually teaches him to use a face-saving façade.

  Remember, overindulgent parents hide problems by giving too much. Mentoring parents offer truth and reality, which in many ways is a greater form of acceptance of their children. A mentoring parent would tell Brad, "I am not buying you anything and I am not keeping any secrets. So, if you do not want to be embarrassed, get better grades". Mentoring parents know that when their children become adults, parents cannot cover-up their adult-children's problems. No employer is going to help an employee cover-up the employee's business failures.

- Put the pocketbook away! I was helping a dad pull away from overindulgence and becoming a mentor to his son. Two months after Christmas his son begged for a new toy while dad was shopping in a department store. Previously, the dad would have conceded defeat to his son's whining. Instead the dad asked a question. He knew his son received about 30 presents for Christmas, two months previously. So he asked, "What was your favorite toy at Christmas time?" His son took a moment to think and his expression told the story. He could not remember any of his Christmas presents.

His dad said to me, "If he cannot remember the toys he got at Christmas time, they are meaningless. If our relationship is based on materialism, our relationship is just as meaningless."

This is a very good point. Put the pocketbook away. In fact, only give your children toys and luxuries for holidays, birthdays and special events. Do not buy them any toys at any other time! Stuff gets in the way of relationships.

⬧ If you blow a gasket and upset your child and you feel guilty, apologize. Do not buy your way out of guilt. If you feel you did something wrong, offer a sincere and heartfelt apology. And, put your pocketbook away!

Parents Who Remind Too Much

Parents who remind too much have the beautiful quality of encouragement, constantly reminding and encouraging their children to behave. But one essential ingredient is missing with their reminders: discipline. Parents, who remind too much, offer too many warnings to their children without backing up their warnings with discipline. They constantly repeat phrases such as, "If you don't stop that I'll…" or "If I told you once, I told you a thousand times…"

Children of "reminder" parents ignore their parents because they know their parents never discipline. A lack of discipline offers children a lack of parenting, which forces children to create their own parenting. This allows children to 'take charge' of their families. So, parents, who remind too much, create children who become powerful, but ineffective leaders of their families.

Children want adults to "take charge"! Here's a great example:

> When I was a school psychologist, an inexperienced eighth-grade teacher lost control of her classroom. What a sight! Twenty-five eighth-graders out of control! The teacher asked me to meet with these children, without her present. The teacher forewarned that there were three ringleaders in the class. They were "in-charge" of her classroom.
>
> I gathered the students in a circle and they sat quietly as I asked my first question: "What do you kids want?" This question met fifteen minutes of silence, which is a very long time with silent eighth-graders. Finally, one of the ringleaders pierced the silence when he said, "Structure, we want structure. I am tired of carrying this class on my shoulders!" I almost fell off my chair. I know children want adults to give them structure, but to hear one admit it in front of his friends was astounding.

Their need for structure was strong, as it is with all children. Their teacher reminded them to behave, but never disciplined them. This is happening in many overindulgent families. Overindulgent parents transfer their power to children who provide the family structure. Scary!

How does this happen? Consider this example:

A two-year-old boy sat with his parents in a restaurant. When his food came, his parents asked him, "Honey, who do you want to feed you? Mommy or Daddy?" The boy pointed at Daddy, and Mommy looked relieved. After dinner, his parents asked him, "Who do you want to clean you? Mommy or Daddy?" He pointed to Daddy, and Mommy looked relieved. When they were about to leave they asked him, "Who do you want to carry you? Mommy or Daddy?" He pointed at Mommy, and Daddy looked relieved. With these simple questions, his parents put him in the power-seat of their family. They were essentially asking him to create the family structure.

Although his parents forced their young boy to be the decision-maker of the family, he was too young to know which parent was too tired or too stressed. That is a parent's job. His parents can better decide who should take care of him at any given moment. By asking him these questions, the power shifts within this family. When power shifts from parents to children too early in life, it creates problems down the road. Bigger concerns arise as children, who become the leaders of their families, become older and their issues become more complex.

⌒╫⌐

Duane, a fourteen-year-old boy, was quite aggressive. When he hit his brother, his parents reminded him to behave, but never disciplined him. Undisciplined, he naturally started hitting other children. In fact, he really enjoyed hitting his smaller buddy, Jim. Duane's mother continually warned Duane to stop hurting Jim. Duane ignored his mother and continued to hit Jim. His mother warned Duane again, but never disciplined him. Duane was becoming a bully and his much smaller buddy, Jim, grew tired of it.

One day Duane was coasting down the sidewalk on his bicycle. Jim positioned himself at the other end of the sidewalk and waited. Finally he saw Duane. Jim called Duane every nasty word he knew. Duane burned with anger and sped after Jim on his bike. Jim ran between two houses, through his grandmother's backyard, to a deck attached to the back of his grandmother's house. Jim ran under the deck and grabbed a rope. His cousin, Marty, who was hiding in a nearby shed, held the other end of the rope. They pulled. Duane flew through the backyard at full speed, hit the rope and flipped off his bicycle, crashing into the gravel.

Duane's parents did not teach him that the "real world" will discipline his bad behavior, and the "real world" may not care about fairness or Duane's safety.

Why would parents weaken their parenting role by only reminding their children to behave, without reinforcing it with discipline? Here are several possible answers.

The Loving but Overindulgent Beliefs of Parents Who Remind Too Much:

1. Some parents, who remind too much, enjoy giving the gift of encouragement to their children, which is a beautiful quality. This becomes a problem when parents, who remind too much, never take any disciplinary action. Why? They want to be buddies with their children and they fear discipline will hurt their buddy relationship.

   Here is a great thought! Children, who have reminder parents, know exactly how many warnings they will get before their parents give-up in frustration. That is amazing! One child proved this theory by frustrating his mother in a counseling session. He quietly counted her reminders, until his mother finally screamed in frustration. He smiled! When parents offer no discipline, it leaves their children "in-charge"—and they know they are "in-charge."

2. Other parents, who remind too much, lack assertiveness. They do not possess the skills of influence and action in many avenues of their life, including parenting. These parents lack assertiveness with their spouses, bosses, in-laws, and others. They hope their children and others will be responsive to their words of encouragement to behave and cooperate. Rarely do they take any assertive actions, including disciplining their children.

3. "If my children do not need to be disciplined, then I am a good parent." This is the belief of some parents, who remind too much. They do not discipline their children, because they believe that if their children do not need discipline, they are good parents. Conversely, if their children need discipline, they feel like bad parents. So, their lack of discipline proves to them they are good parents.

4. A few parents, who remind too much, just do not believe in discipline. They believe that discipline harms the natural development of children. If they impose the limits of discipline, their children will not develop into what nature intended them to be. I always give these parents the assignment of reading the book *Lord of the Flies*. Remember, most of us read this book in High School? The children were stranded on an island and parented themselves. They created chaos.

Commentary

When there is little guidance from parents, children develop problems. In his four short years, Jeffrey knew his mother was a "reminder" parent because he knew discipline would never happen. His mother constantly encouraged Jeffrey to behave, with Jeffrey ignoring her. He did what he pleased, seizing the powerful leadership role of his family. His mother never disciplined Jeffrey, which was unfortunate, because one of the goals of parenting is to prepare children for the real world.

When Jeffrey entered preschool, his teacher warned him once, and immediately disciplined Jeffrey when he failed to behave. Because discipline was new to him, Jeffrey had a tantrum. He did not know how to react to appropriate discipline. Jeffrey's parents did not prepare him for the real world, including the real experience of discipline at school.

Consider these suggestions to stop being a parent who reminds too much:

♦ A great parenting technique for parents, who remind too much, is "one warning and a discipline". Be completely consistent with this idea. Offer one warning and then discipline. When you offer the limits of "one warning and then a discipline" you are teaching your children balance. Without balance, life becomes miserable.

♦ Parents who are reluctant to discipline their children want to be buddies with their children. This is impossible! Buddies do not discipline their buddies. Buddies are not legally responsible for their buddies. Buddies always believe their buddies. Parents do discipline their children. They are legally responsible for their children. And sometimes parents need to be skeptical of their children's honesty.

It is a beautiful thing to be a buddy when your children become adults. When raising children, the role of the mentoring parent is too complicated to reduce itself to a buddy-relationship.

Parents Who Wear Blinders

Parents who wear blinders have the incredible quality of accurately recognizing the good in people. They correctly understand their children's good qualities and appropriately praise their children. This admirable quality becomes distorted as parents with "blinders" ignore their children's flaws. So, parents with "blinders" appropriately compliment their children for their positive attributes, but never give their children a correct appraisal of their flaws. As a result, they fail to teach their children how to improve their flaws.

When parents do not correct their children's flaws, many overindulged children believe they have no flaws. They come to believe they are perfect! This gives children an inflated self-esteem with a strong self-centered attitude. If there are no flaws to correct, children do not learn valuable life experiences and the skills to manage life. Instead, they become over-dependent on their parents, and never develop self-reliance or the skills necessary for mutual relationships.

Benny was bright and loved learning. His parents realized Benny was bright and they appropriately encouraged him to learn. On entrance to kindergarten, his parents had no doubt Benny would be successful throughout his school years. One of the first lessons his teacher discussed was the concept of sharing. Benny hated sharing, and his parents never corrected this flaw. Benny decided that a classroom paintbrush was his paintbrush. When a classmate decided to use the same paintbrush, Benny felt justified in dumping paint over his classmate's head.

Thelma's mother always praised Thelma's intelligence, and her praise was justified. Thelma was bright. In her first year of high school, Thelma was at the top of her class. Thelma also had natural leadership qualities, exemplified by the way her friends admired her and followed her example. When a new girl entered Thelma's high school, Thelma had options. She could easily help the new student gain acceptance with Thelma's friends. Instead, Thelma nastily ridiculed this new student, and her friends followed her lead.

Thelma had a strong need for false-status, which her parents never corrected. Because Thelma saw this new student as a threat to her status, she ridiculed the new student instead of helping her find acceptance. Thelma had a great potential for a beautiful skill (offering acceptance), but she had an uncorrected flaw (a need for false-status at the expense of others).

Both Thelma and Benny had fantastic skills, but their parents never corrected their flaws. In both cases, the parents accurately praised their children's strengths, but failed to guide their children out of their flaws.

Why would parents, with blinders, accurately compliment their children, but ignore their children's real flaws?

The Loving but Overindulgent Beliefs of Parents With Blinders:

1. Many parents, with blinders, believe they will harm their children if they discipline them. They believe that to create good self-esteem within their children, their children should receive only positive messages. This complicates the lives of overindulged children, as they eventually go to school, where both teachers and classmates give them more realistic appraisals of positive attributes and flaws.

   "Blinders" parents believe they are helping their children by never mentioning these flaws. But, they miss many opportunities to help their children grow and develop. When the real world readily points out obvious flaws, these children are shocked. Instead of learning to correct their flaws, they react with hostility, anger, and for a few—rage.

2. Some parents, with blinders, do not see any flaws within their children. They believe that flaws do not exist in their children, so there is nothing to correct. They believe that nature gave them a perfect child.

   Thelma's mother believed Thelma was flawless. When she learned about Thelma's fight with the new student, her mother immediately assumed the information was false. She refused to believe that her child would be so nasty, which prevented her from correcting her daughter's behavior.

3. Just as with the parent who reminds too much, some parents with blinders feel tremendous competition with other parents. To have an edge, they readily see the good in their own children, and quickly spot the bad in other children. When Thelma had her conflict with the

new student, her mother believed there was a real problem: she insisted that this new student created the conflict. She rationalized with the school counselor "Thelma was not in any conflicts before this new student arrived."

Consider these suggestions to stop being a parent with blinders:

+ Always remember, if you edit out your children's flaws you are rejecting a part of your child. It is natural that all children have flaws. But, overindulgent parents are exceptionally skilled at ignoring their children's flaws. Directly deal with your children's flaws. One of the biggest jobs of parenting is to correct your children's flaws so they become better adults. If they are not corrected in childhood, their adult-life becomes very complicated.

+ Parents, who remind too much, believe that discipline will harm their children. I want you to know that appropriate discipline will never harm your children. Think carefully about your children and how you would discipline them. My best suggestion is to love your children equally, but discipline them differently.

When my wife and I first started parenting, we used time-outs with both of our children. For children, the most boring place in our home was the big blue chair in our bedroom. When we put our youngest son in time-out, time-out was helpful because he was very physically active. But, our oldest son was a thinker. Time-out was not effective for him, as he would sit and contemplate the world. But, restricting computer time worked well.

So, it is important to deeply consider your children's personality when planning discipline. One foundational question is, "Is it better to restrict their favorite activities or to calm them with time-outs". Always remember that discipline has the potential to create positive emotions within your children. Our active son, who is now an adult, loves that old blue chair.

Parents Who Glorify Too Much

Parents who glorify too much have the wonderful quality of complimenting others. "Glorifying" parents are similar to parents with "blinders," as they ignore their children's flaws; however, "glorifying" parents have one striking difference. "Blinders" parents have an accurate understanding of their children's talents. "Glorifying" parents exaggerate their children's talents or see incredible qualities within their children that do not really exist. "Glorifying" parents exaggerate their children's talents and ignore their children's flaws. In essence, they do not accept any part of their children.

Their children mystify parents, who glorify their children. They believe that everything their children touch turns to gold. They believe their children have the best personalities, the best jobs, and the best friends. Their children are the best of all.

Julie constantly bragged about her children. In her mind, her children had no equals. If her teenager got a job, no matter how menial, it was the best job in the world. When her adult-children bought a home, there was no equal to that new residence.

To glorify her children, Julie would gloss over real problems. Some of her children became so self-centered they had few friendships at school. One of her children was convicted of a felon, selling drugs to minors. Julie's adult-children had incredible debt, but she never mentioned it. Julie swept these problems out of her mind.

When her friends discussed their children, Julie immediately geared into competition by bragging about her children. Her need for competition was strong. So strong that Julie lost friendships because she could not enjoy the successes of her friends' children.

One of Julie's daughters, Cara, had serious problems at school. Cara was perplexed about why many of her classmates wanted to fight with her. Like her mother, Cara had a habit of bragging, and would readily point out the flaws of others, embarrassing her classmates. Unlike her mother, Cara's classmates did not glorify Cara. Instead, they viewed her as obnoxious. Being children, they did not handle this problem well, and fought with Cara.

Cara's glorification, by her mother, led Cara to believe she was perfect. But, the real world did not accept Cara's glorified image. By distorting Cara's view of herself, Julie did not prepare Cara to manage life.

Why would parents glorify their children?

The Overindulgent Beliefs of Parents
Who Glorify Their Children:

1. Some parents, who glorify their children, feel they are living a mundane life. Because they are disappointed with their life, they want to glorify some part of their life. Their children are easy targets for glorification. Julie, Cara's mother, needs a life with real purpose, a life that gives her meaning. Her purpose in life could be parenting, but to do a complete job of parenting she needs to address Cara's real flaws. Instead, Julie helped Cara create a self-centered attitude.

2. In other families, one parent glorifies their children, while the other parent has a realistic view. This creates real complications. To children, the "glorifying" parent appears to be the better parent, while the more realistic parent seems too critical.

   Jerry and Diane had three children. Jerry would often glorify their children and refused to acknowledge their flaws. Diane had a more accurate view of her children. She loved her children enough to look at their flaws and help them make corrections. Jerry could not do this. He continued to glorify his children, while Diane addressed their real concerns.

   As Diane would approach her children to address real concerns, Jerry intervened. He stopped Diane from helping their children correct their flaws, painting a picture of Diane as the nasty parent and promoting himself as the nice parent. Jerry manipulated their relationship into a competition, getting his children to align with him.

   Jerry and Diane eventually divorced. Jerry became a holiday parent showering the children with toys and fun activities. Diane continued to help her children with their real concerns. As their children matured into adult life, they developed a more meaningful relationship with Diane, who always offered the truth to her children. Eventually, most children know what they need and come to appreciate parents who give them honest and quality lessons in life.

Commentary

Because we love our children, it is easy to glorify them. But if we have an unrealistic view of our children, we create self-inflated, egocentric children. Let me share an example:

I once counseled a girl named Nicki, who was a nice child, but not gifted. Her parents glorified her and always called her gifted. When she entered school, her parents convinced Nicki that she would easily be at the top of her class. When it became obvious that her skills were average, Nicki's parents placed more pressure on her to succeed. When Nicki received grades that were less than "A" quality, she became disruptive in her classroom with tears and tantrums.

Nicki accepted her parents' unrealistic belief. This inaccurate assessment—that she was gifted—hurt her honest understanding of herself, and manifested itself in unacceptable behavior. She was not ready for the real world that honestly told her, "Hey Nicki, you are a great person, but you have average intelligence." Nicki needed her parents to mentor with truth and honesty.

Consider these suggestions to stop being a parent that glorifies:

* When parents glorify their children, they reject their children. They are not accepting their children as they really are. This is one of the main reasons children disconnect from their parents. Parents, who glorify, create images of their children that are not real. It is impossible to create a bond with an image. So, children distance themselves from parents.

  To realistically discover your children's strengths and flaws, allow them to explore. Glorifying parents expect too much from their children. Remember one of the first stories in this book, about the mom who bought her son a $32,000 guitar? She glorified her son by believing he would be the next Jimmy Hendrix. But, this mom actually restricted her son's ability to explore his interests. She invested so much money into her glorified belief about her son's talents that she had no further money. She should have bought him a $32.00 guitar. If he truly progressed with the guitar over the next year, she could encourage him with a $150.00 guitar. By investing $32,000 she stopped her ability to help him explore his talents. Like many children, he may play the guitar for a week and then move on to another interest.

  Allow your children to explore by letting them test their talents. Make small investments in their talents. When you see a talent surface, make gradual investments to encourage your children.

Parents Who Play Favorites

Parents who play favorites have the excellent qualities of preference and discrimination, but they distort these qualities by preferring only one of their children. Their preferential overindulgence of one child is so extreme that they neglect their other children, who realize they are not favored and become angry. What's interesting is that, as young children, they rarely become angry with the parent who is playing favorites. Instead, they become angry with the favored child.

Jamie was the oldest and preferred child in her family of three children. It was obvious to her sister and brother that their mother preferred Jamie. Her mother always laughed harder when Jamie told a funny story, and cried harder when Jamie was hurt. Jamie's brother and sister recall countless memories of Jamie getting more attention, affection, activities, gifts, and everything.

Not only did Jamie's brother and sister become angry with Jamie; they also detached from their mother. As this problem grew into adulthood, every holiday, birthday, and special family event became a time of conflict. As Jamie's brother and sister became adults, they found their attempts to build relationships with Jamie and their mother fruitless.

⚬━⚯

In another example, Ruth's children were adults. It was obvious that she preferred her youngest daughter above the rest of her children. She showered her favored daughter with attention, advice, and money. Lots of money! In fact, Ruth's daughter had a home

*with all the trimmings, paid for by Ruth. Ruth also
gave advice to her favored daughter and son-in-law.
Lots of advice! Marital advice, financial advice,
child-rearing advice, and even advice about sex. Too
much advice! But Ruth's daughter and son-in-law
never complained to Ruth, because they were too
financially dependent on her.*

Why would parents play favorites at the expense of
their other children?

The Overindulgent Beliefs Parents
Who Play Favorites:

1. Some parents, who play favorites, over-connect with
   the preferred child. For example, a shy parent may
   over-connect with the child who is too shy or with the
   child who is very social. This over-connection promotes a strong attachment between parent and child,
   which does not occur with the other children.

   Sometimes a parent may have a favorite hobby (such
   as dance, football, or soccer) and the child who excels
   in this preferred hobby becomes the favored child.

   Whatever the link, these parents naturally favor one
   child above the rest.

   Jamie's mother was shy, and Jamie's social gregari-
   ousness was extremely attractive to her. As a result,
   Jamie's mother attained a life she always wanted, but
   she was living it through Jamie. This vicarious life
   became so enticing that she ignored her other children.

2. Other parents, who play favorites, recognize that one of
   their children is vulnerable. They assume that their
   other children do not need as much special care and
   attention as the vulnerable child does—but they do.

Ruth had many children, but she only showered excessive finances and advice on one child, who was the daughter Ruth believed incapable of managing life. Ruth assumed that her other children were more able to handle their problems and frustrations. Actually, they were more able, not because they were innately brighter, but because they learned through Ruth's neglect to not depend on others. When Ruth's other children became more independent, she assumed they did not need her. Ruth believed she was only useful to the child who was incapable. Of course, Ruth had much more than money to offer her children, but rarely did.

3. Some "favoritism" parents are emotionally needy. The children who respond best to their parents' neediness get the favored attention. Children learn, mostly by trial and error, how to get their parents' attention, and those children who better read and respond to their parents' needs often become favored children. The children who do not respond to their parents' needs receive less attention.

4. A few "favoritism" parents are replaying their own parents' tendency to show favoritism. Parents, not favored in childhood, create preferences when they become parents. When a "favoritism" parent prefers one child, the favored child usually offers that parent favoritism in return. Although these parents were least favored when they were children, they are now in-charge of dispensing and receiving favoritism. They decide who the favored child is and is not. In at least the eyes of one child, these parents become favored, a status they could not win in childhood.

Consider this suggestion to stop being a parent that plays favorites:

Favoritism is one of the most destructive family dynamics, because most "favoritism" parents do not realize they are playing favorites. Therefore, favoritism may last for a lifetime, as children become adults and still compete for their parents' attention. Without counseling, favoritism continues to breed serious family problems. It is vital that parents, who play favorites, get individual and family counseling.

Parents Who Blame Too Much

Parents who blame too much have the beautiful quality of protecting their children; however, they believe they are protecting their children by always blaming others for their children's misbehavior. For example, if a teacher has a conflict with a child, "blaming" parents immediately side with their child and blame the teacher. They do not suspend judgment until they talk to the teacher, but immediately believe their children and readily blame any opposing party. They rarely consider their children's responsibility for any conflict.

Parents, who blame too much, are renowned for blaming one teacher for destroying their children's lives or blame other children for ruining special events. The result is that children, led to believe they are blameless, never learn to manage life's problems. Instead, they learn to blame others.

Ally knew she slacked off on her studies in her last semester of her senior year, putting her college scholarship in jeopardy. She knew she was failing calculus and it was her fault. Instead of telling her parents she was responsible, she started to monster-build her calculus teacher. She would spend many hours complaining about her calculus teacher's unfairness and favoritism toward other students. She even told her parents that her calculus teacher changed grades for certain favored students, which was a lie. When Ally's parents received Ally's grades, their anger ignited because they knew Ally had lost her scholarship. But they were not angry with Ally. They were enraged with Ally's calculus teacher.

Believing everything that Ally said about her calculus teacher, they tried to force the school principal to fire the teacher. To this day they blame the teacher for Ally's loss of her scholarship. The teacher gave Ally the grade she earned. The teacher was doing his job!

⌒⫮⌒

At another school, on senior day, high school seniors attacked their school building and destroyed school property. The school administration realized these seniors displayed unpredictable violent behavior, so the administration barred them from graduation ceremonies. Several parents were upset with the school administration's discipline, but they understood their children deserved this tough consequence. Other parents said, "Not attending graduation ceremonies will scar my child's self-esteem for life." These parents became angry at the school administration, claiming that their discipline was too harsh.

Why would parents blame others and never correctly see their children's responsibility for a bad experience or conflict?

*The Overindulgent Beliefs of Parents
Who Blame Too Much:*

1. If there is a problem within a family and the family blames someone outside their family, the family is off the hook. The family never has to consider their contribution to any problems. It makes them feel more comfortable to blame someone else, instead of taking responsibility in life. So, they never change.

   When parents blame others, they avoid personal responsibility and the discomfort of change. Parents, who blame too much, rarely hold their children responsible for their actions. For example, instead of getting upset with their children for attacking the school, "blaming" parents assume the school administration was too harsh. They rarely consider, "If sixteen seniors came to my home and destroyed my property, would I want them to come to a special celebration in my home, one week later?" Instead, they inaccurately conclude, "My child's self-esteem will crumble if he (or she) cannot attend high school graduation." This is not true. Their self-esteem will not crumble. If these seniors lose their attendance at high school graduation, and parents reinforce the discipline by saying, "You earned this consequence," these seniors will learn to behave.

2. Some "blaming" parents have an unusual strain of the "glorifying" parent. They glorify their children, believing their children are too perfect to be responsible for any problem. These parents automatically assume that if their children misbehave, there are valid reasons. Ally's parents viewed her as too perfect to lie about her calculus teacher, although she did. Her parents' overindulgent belief of Ally's perfection led them to

assume that Ally was telling the truth, preventing them from accepting her calculus teacher as a valid source of information. This, of course, stopped her parents from getting at the truth, which stopped them from changing Ally's lying and manipulation.

Commentary

When parents blame others, they promote the illusion of the 'bad guy,' which is a person who is completely bad. I equate it to an old Gene Autry western from the 1950s, where the bad guys were completely bad. They had no good features, so it was permissible for the hero to do whatever was necessary to save the day.

"Blaming" parents automatically create a completely bad picture of anyone who is in conflict with their children. This allows "blaming" parents to feel justified in taking any action to rescue their children. "Blaming" parents are not teaching children that conflict is a two-way street, with responsibility for all involved.

Consider these suggestions to stop being a parent who blames too much:

♦ Here is my best suggestion when there is a conflict between your child and a teacher or anyone else. Do a "Round- Up"! For example, when teachers send failure notices many children "monster build " about their teacher. When you hear this "monster building" immediately contact the teacher and set up a meeting (a Round Up). Get your child and teacher in the same room, have an open mind and the truth usually surfaces.

♦ I got in a little trouble when I was in middle school. My dad wanted the truth. So, he sat me down and asked me 100 questions about the incident. I lied through my teeth! I was convincing and he looked convinced. A week later he asked me the same 100 questions. I could not remember what I told him. He pierced me with these words, "A liar always forgets!" He was right. The truth is the truth and should not change. If you want to know if your children are telling you the truth, ask them 100 questions, wait a week and ask again.

♦ Once you have determined the truth and if your child is at fault, allow consequences to happen. If you discover your child actually failed a class, let the failure happen. If you learn that your child did not graduate, make your child take an extra seminar to complete high school. Follow through with the consequences.

The "Overly-Responsible" Parent

As with "blaming" parents, "overly-responsible" parents have the valuable quality of protection, but they have a different way of distorting it. "Overly-responsible" parents do not blame others for their children's misbehaviors. Instead, they always blame themselves.

When they blame themselves, they stop their children from taking responsibility for their actions. In fact, if "overly-responsible" parents believe they are the cause of their children's misbehavior, they see no reason to discipline their children. This allows their children to continue to misbehave, without correction.

Glenda constantly made excuses for her son, Kenny. Every time he misbehaved she said, "It's my fault Kenny is like that." So, Kenny did anything he pleased. If he wanted something, he would steal it. If a child was in his way, he pushed the child. He spouted off to his teacher. No matter what he did, his mother would say, "It's my fault Kenny is like that." All children misbehave, so it is not Glenda's fault every time Kenny misbehaves.

But self-blame does have a self-fulfilling prophecy. It is Glenda's fault if Kenny's misbehavior continues undisciplined, as Glenda keeps explaining, "It's my fault Kenny is like that." At some point, Glenda's unwillingness to discipline will be responsible for Kenny's continued misbehavior.

~⚜~

"If I had not gotten divorced, he would not be in this trouble today," Roberta said, after her son was arrested for shoplifting. She never held him responsible for his actions, because she continually blamed herself. She only held herself responsible because she believed that her decision to divorce ruined her son's life. Although I would love to see divorce go away, if it were true that divorce created crime, imagine how many children would be in prison. There are many children, with divorced parents, who never consider committing a crime. Divorce does not help, but it is not solely responsible for criminal behavior. Her son is making bad decisions and needs to be disciplined.

Why would parents blame themselves and not hold their children responsible for their misbehavior?

The Overindulgent Beliefs of "Overly-Responsible" Parents:

1. Some "overly-responsible" parents were scapegoats in their own childhood families. Their families continually blamed them for every problem when they were children. So they continue to accept this role with their own family, always taking responsibility for their children's misbehavior.

   When Glenda was a child, she was the family scapegoat. As she grew up, taking blame was a way of life. She naturally continued her self-blaming as she raised her son, feeling responsible for his misbehavior.

   Often parents, who self-blame, place too much importance on one reason (such as divorce) and never consider the full picture. Every time her son misbehaved, Glenda would not consider the full picture of all the reasons that contributed to her son's misbehavior. Instead, she only blamed herself, and never disciplined him. So, he never changed.

2. Becoming a mentoring parent is a commitment that requires making at least some changes in lifestyle. Some parents are fearful of making changes. For them, there is safety in blaming themselves for their children's misbehavior, as it is a parenting style that does not require change. They just continue with the unchanging thought, "It is all my fault."

3. Some "overly responsible" parents have the belief, "If I take responsibility, I am helping my child." This belief offers a false sense of empowerment. When a parent

takes the blame for a child's misbehavior, that child feels relief. An "overly-responsible" parent feels empowered when his or her child feels this relief. It is false empowerment. Although the child feels relief, he or she does not learn to change his or her behavior.

This was the problem with divorced Roberta, whose son shoplifted. She believed that if she took the blame, she gave relief to her son. In reality, she was losing control of him.

Consider these suggestions to stop blaming yourself:

• We feel guilt as soon as our children are born. Guilt is very natural for parents. So keep your guilt in check! Always consider the full picture. Roberta blamed herself for her son's stealing because she divorced his father. I counseled Roberta to consider the full picture. I told her many children come from divorced families that never steal. I wanted Roberta to widen her view of her child to realize that he was making bad decisions. And, she needed to give him consequences instead of excuses.

• Beware of the illusion of false-relief. Your children should not feel relief when they misbehavior, which they will if you consume the blame. There is good tension, and being uncomfortable with misbehavior is a good tension for children to experience.

The "Ultimately Responsible" Parent

"Ultimately responsible" parents offer a different twist, which is confusing to children. "Ultimately responsible" parents unpredictably explode with anger. They rage at their children. Later they feel bad and take it all back by blaming themselves. This confuses children who become tense, especially when discussing any family issues that might ignite emotions. They are fearful their parents will rage again, and these children will do anything to avoid their parents' tirade. These exploding parents stop families from discussing emotionally sensitive issues. After the tirade, their caring nature makes these parents feel guilty. They overcompensate by overindulging their children, hoping to repair the damage created by their tirade.

> *Tim had a bad temper, made worse by its unpredictability. Usually he was calm, but occasionally he severely exploded without warning. Most of the time, Tim was a good father, but just when his children started feeling comfortable around him, his anger unexpectedly exploded. Afterwards, guilt-ridden, he took his children shopping at their favorite toy store, where he overindulged them. But he never fixed his anger, nor did he teach his children that they were not the source of his anger. Instead, he overindulged them.*

Why would parents angrily blame their children, and then try to overcompensate by overindulging their children?

The Overindulgent Beliefs of "Ultimately Responsible" Parents

1. Passivity is one issue. Some "ultimately responsible" parents are so passive that they do not manage their lives. They lack assertiveness, allowing others to mistreat them. This mistreatment creates a brewing anger within them. By not asserting themselves, "ultimately responsible" parents become frustrated and eventually explode. They unleash their anger on their children, who are safe targets. Since they often realize (after the blow up) their children are not the real source of their anger, they try to repair the damage by overindulging their children.

2. Some "ultimately responsible" parents are legitimately angry with their children, but do not express their anger well. Instead of learning to appropriately dialogue about their upset feelings, they withhold their hurts, which brews and festers. Of course, these brewing emotions eventually ignite into rage.

Suggestions for "Ultimately Responsible" Parents

Without assertiveness, life becomes frustrating. One common feature of people who lack assertiveness is that they harbor considerable anger. Their anger grows as others, including loved ones, continue to take advantage of them.

Parents, with frustrated anger coupled with non-assertiveness, may release their anger toward safe targets—their children. These unpredictable explosions create insecure children.

Because nonassertive parents have brewing anger, any minor conflict can result in a raging outburst. When these outbursts occur, children learn to restrain their emotions, avoid managing conflicts, and never discuss emotional issues. The problem escalates when children become teenagers, since most teenagers experience at least one big emotional issue they will need to manage. It is vital that people, harboring anger, gain counseling services. Children will not bond with angry parents.

Summary

Love your children, but put your pocket book away! The message of this chapter is that there is so much more to parenting than making children artificially happy. Happiness derives from many sources. One major contribution is parents who teach children to manage life. Life management creates capable children who have balance in every part of life.

~ CHAPTER 2 ~

What Overindulgent Parents Believe

What pushes parents into overindulging their children? Why are they convinced they are doing the best for their children with excessive giving and too much permission?

There are parenting beliefs that overindulgent parents hold dear. They are convinced that these beliefs will lead them to a loving relationship with their children. Unfortunately, I do not believe these beliefs are helpful because they create more problems than solutions for parents.

The more you know about the following overindulgent beliefs, the more you can resist them. Consider each of the following overindulgent parenting beliefs carefully. These beliefs convince many parents they will achieve greater bonding with their children. These distorted parenting beliefs do not work.

Overindulgent Belief # 1: Constant Happiness

Overindulgent parents believe they can enhance their children's self-esteem by keeping their children constantly happy. Parents with this belief have two goals:

1. They push their children to be constantly happy.

2. They stop their children from experiencing any uncomfortable emotions.

It is admirable for parents to want to enhance their children's self-esteem. But, overindulgent parents believe in the marketing definition of *quick-fix happiness,* which suggests that being a good parent equals the number of happy experiences parents provide for their children. This *quick-fix happiness* drives parents to fill every conceivable hour in a child's day with happiness.

If you push a constant stream of happy experiences onto your children, you will be disillusioned with the outcome. When parents obsessively focus on their children's happiness, their parenting becomes constricted and ineffective. They believe their sole purpose, as a parent, is to constantly pursue *quick-fix happiness* for their children.

I counseled two loving parents who were classic overindulgers. They sent their son to a "fun" daycare. Several times a week, they scheduled "happy" activities. For example, they took him to McDonald's almost every weekend for a Happy Meal. They believed these happy activities would build his self-esteem.

When their son entered school, he had serious behavior problems. It became obvious that his parents missed vital ingredients in their parenting! Their son was so self-centered he had not learned to share, cooperate, sacrifice, or take turns with other children. His parents were so focused on making him happy, he lost many opportunities to learn the skills needed to manage life. Instead, he became an expert in the art of gaining overindulgence.

Why would parents constantly push a quick-fix "marketing" definition of happiness onto their children?

1. Buying happiness is a parental obsession! In our American culture, quickly acquiring happiness items like toys, fun activities, and Happy Meals is easy, convenient, and quick! Parents do not have to drive far to purchase "happy moments" for their children. Parents, buying "happy moments", convince themselves they offer deeply invested parenting. But they don't, which is disappointing to children. Children are enticed by these "happy moments", but they would rather have a real relationship with their parents.

2. A common theme in today's culture is Burger King's slogan, "Have it your way." Many adults want happiness in every part of their lives (career, money, advancement, expensive cars, marriages, and children). "I want" is the American dream of our times. When applied to parenting, "I want" does not work as an effective parenting style.

I recently sat in a stunning park in Santa Monica. I was impressed as it was filled with young children delightfully playing together, with parents watching and playing with them. I thought, "What a gorgeous memory for these children." As two young girls ran in front of me, one of them said, "I'll ask my nanny." Suddenly I realized these were not parents creating memories with their children. They were all nannies!

∾

In a related story, a successful agent arrived at home one evening to find his daughter stumbled and scraped her knee. He knelt down and opened his

*arms to her. She ran passed him and into the arms of
her nanny. He painfully realized that his daughter did
not see him as a source of comfort!*

Some overindulgent parents believe their children exist
to fulfill the needs of parents. Rarely do parents with "I
want" attitudes think about what is best for children before
having children. Instead, they believe they can work their
children into their busy "I want" lifestyles. They convince
themselves that if they make their children happy, they are
good parents. They leave their children with a nice nanny,
send their children to a happy daycare, and give them many
happy activities, allowing parents to limit their own involvement with their children.

Purchasing "happy moments" releases parents from
their personal responsibility of raising their children. Parents continue with their "I want" lifestyle, falsely believing
their children are happy. Unfortunately, by the time their
children become teenagers, they often detach from their
parents, ripe for problems that demand considerable
parental attention.

Giving the responsibility of raising their children to
others, gives absentee parents a built-in scapegoat. Parents,
who blame too much, allow substitutes to raise their children. If their children have behavior problems, the
substitutes are held responsible. Parents are off the hook!

Many "I want" parents say they both need to work to
provide a good home to raise happy children. They are
absent from their home to financially support their good
home. Their need to support their new home justifies send-
ing their children away from their home to a daycare or
baby-sitter, without realizing the implications or the irony
of this action. Lets define a "good home" through the eyes
of an overindulgent parent.

Many parents, of this generation, have "Empty House Syndrome". In other words, they are living above their financial means. They stretch their budgets to have a huge and beautiful house, they really cannot afford. This forces them to spend more time pursuing money for a house payment than pursuing quality time with their children.

Some families have such low incomes that both parents need to work to survive. Survival is the priority. But there are many two-parent families with good incomes who want the extra income that two careers offer. Whatever the reason, the results are often the same. Without at least one parent actively engaged in parenting, children do not have the benefits of a mentoring parent.

Consider the unique gifts that only you can offer your children. For example, let's pretend that I am your child's daycare worker. One day your child scrapes a knee and cries in agony. As the daycare worker, I could hug your upset child ten times and those ten hugs would not be as healing as one hug from you. The caress of your familiar embrace heals your child's pain. One little piece of genuine happiness you can easily give your children is that they know you will be there when they experience physical or emotional pain. Parenting needs to happen when a child needs parenting. No substitute can replace this special bond.

How do children react to parents who constantly push the marketing definition of happiness?

Parents hope their children will react to overindulgence with thoughts like, "Wow, this is great! I love and appreciate my parents!" This rarely happens. Instead, children usually respond with feelings of entitlement and resentment.

Instead of learning genuine happiness through a strong bond with parents, overindulged children demand more fun activities, greater leniencies, and pressure parents for more luxuries. They become overindulgent beneficiaries and expect constant attention and entitlement. They eventually have the same expectations of their school and community. Their resentment also ignites. Whenever a child is over-dependent on a parent, resentment brews. Of course, this is not what overindulgent parents want. These caring parents become perplexed by their children's strong feelings of enti-tlement ("I want more ...") and resentment ("... and I'm angry about it").

I can tell you from years of coaching and counseling families, overindulgence does not create happy children. Consider this next overindulgent belief.

Overindulgent Belief # 2: "Whatever You Want!"

Overindulgent parents believe that uncondi-tional love means children should receive whatever they want and do whatever they want.

Parents who embrace this overindulgent belief have two major concerns:

1. They have difficulty saying "No" to their children. In fact, they measure how good they are as parents by how many times they say "Yes" to their children. They believe that being a good parent includes buying, giv-ing, leniency, entertaining, and cultivating low expectations for their children.

2. Parents who define unconditional love as "giving" lux-uries and freedoms have difficulty distinguishing between their children's wants (desire for luxuries) and their children's needs (love, affection, honesty, etc.).

Fulfilling "needs" is necessary for quality relationships with children. But, luxuries are never necessary for quality relationships.

Overindulgent parents give in to all of their children's requests, which results in children being in-charge of their families. Parents, harboring the distorted definition of unconditional love as constant "giving", overindulge every whim of their children with luxuries. Parents, risking 18% interest on severe credit card debt, give their children whatever they want. When parents give too much stuff and every freedom, they actual train their children to overburden their parents.

Why would parents accept this excessive "giving" definition of unconditional love?

1. Many parents overindulge their children to prove to themselves and others that they are good parents. They demonstrate their worthiness, by giving their children many luxuries and freedoms.

   They believe that being a good parent means that they are buddies with their children. This "Do Whatever You Want" belief pressures overindulgent parents to believe that a buddy relationship with their children is a bond. They do not realize that being a buddy means they are losing their parental influence.

2. When overindulgent parents say, "Yes" to children, they feel wonderful. They convince themselves they are good parents by saying, "Yes". Overindulgent parents are happiest when their children are smiling after hearing "Yes" to yet another luxury or fun activity.

   On the other hand, children often make a "want" for a luxury sound like a "need." For example, most children ask for their own television in their bedroom. Overindulgent parents have difficulty determining if a television is a "want" or a "need." When parents confuse a "want" and a "need," they become marks for manipulation from spoiled children.

A need is anything that sustains quality relationships: such as love, affection, food, shelter, safety, honesty, hugs. Wants are desires for luxuries: televisions, expensive shoes, designer clothes, stereos, trips to Disneyland, cars, and etcetera. Parents never need to give luxuries to have great relationships with children. The proof for this last statement is that many poor families, who have few luxuries, can have very good relationships. Always remember, showering children with luxuries is not a requirement for good relationships.

How do children react to parents who excessively "give" instead of offering quality parenting?

Children, with parents who give them everything they desire, push for more! Their parents truly love them, but mistakenly believe that excessive giving will prove their love. They hope their children will reciprocate with love. Instead of love, these children demand more luxuries and fun activities. If parents resist, overindulged children become angry.

Children need so much more than luxuries and fun activities from their parents. Children do not always realize that they need love, bonding, discipline, and limits—but they do. They also need to hear the word "No". Clark and Dawson in 1998 also found that overindulged children received little consequences for breaking rules. Without consequences children do no learn limits. In order to place limits on your children, you need to use the word "No" and make it one of the most important words in your vocabulary.

Not only do overindulged children have strong feelings of entitlement, they actively learn skills to convince their parents to continue to overindulge them. When overindulged children hear the word "No," they refuse to accept it. Instead, they sulk, nag, whine, play guilt trips, and generally make life miserable for parents. Many children realize that their overindulgent parents' first "No" is not their final answer. So they whittle their parent's firm "No" into a "Maybe" and eventually into a "Yes."

By saying "No" to your children, they learn to be self-reliant. When you say "No", direct your children to work for what they want. We want children to get what they want in life. But, we want them to work for it. If they do not work for it, they refine their skills of getting what they want from others, without earning it. Instead of self-reliance, they wallow in over-dependency. If this happens, their only coping skill is the attitude: "You get it for me."

Overindulgent Belief # 3: Shielded From Consequences

Overindulgent parents shield their children from the consequences of their children's actions, as well as the complications of life.

Parents who embrace this overindulgent belief have two areas of concern:

1. Overindulgent parents do not understand the concept of "harm's way." Parents should stop their children from life-threatening experiences that may result in

severe physical or psychological consequences (harm's way). Overindulgent parents overcompensate by protecting their children from the consequences of all their actions, harmful or not.

2. Overindulgent parents love to pamper their children. They believe in the "marketing" definition of happiness, suggesting that good self-esteem is the result of keeping their children happy. So, they buffer their children from the consequences of their actions to keep them happy. Since consequences make their children uncomfortable, overindulgent parents harbor the distorted belief that all consequences (even appropriate discipline) create severe psychological harm within their children. This distorted belief drives overindulgent parents to stop their children from receiving consequences for their misbehavior.

Never shield your children from the consequences of their misbehavior. If you do you will create serious problems! If children do not receive consequences for their misbehavior, they will not gain self-guidance. Children create self-guidance when they attach good thinking to their emotions. This good thinking, which promotes self-guidance, needs to come from you.

Consider the example, I used in Chapter 1, of good thinking attached to an uncomfortable emotion. If you are at work and you do something that embarrasses you, you can combine this uncomfortable emotion with good thinking, which helps you conclude "I won't do this again at work." This is self-guidance, which is a self-directed willingness to follow rules. For children, self-guidance influences the development of conscience. If their self-guidance is poorly developed, their conscience is also poorly developed.

School administrators enforced the rule that football players arrested for drinking would have to sit out for several games. The students knew the policy and realized it applied to all students in any school activity. It was a logical rule that enforced the idea that students need to use good self-guidance. Their commitment to the team included a commitment to the school's "No Drinking" policy.

When parents heard the school administration's decision to follow this policy, they went through the roof! Many parents came to school board meetings with attorneys, to fight the policy. The argument these parents used was, "You are hurting my child's self-esteem with your harsh policy." These parents did not understand the concept of "harm's way."

"Harm's way" is an important parenting principle. Overindulgent parents buffer children from the consequences of their actions because they believe it will hurt their children's self-esteem. In reality, these parents are putting their children in "harm's way." If the parents of drinking football players successfully eliminate the school's consequences, they will teach their teenagers that they can continue to drink alcohol without consequences.

If parents buffer their children from the consequences of their actions, children see no reason to change their misbehavior. They will not create self-guidance that says, "Hey, I better not do that." Instead, overindulged children learn, "I can do what I want and my parents will rescue me from the consequences of my actions." Parents who encourage this attitude are setting their children up for a bigger fall in life, and are putting their children in "harm's way." Without guidance from parents, who enforce consequences, these children will not develop a conscience!

Why would parents buffer their children from the consequences of their misbehavior?

1. It is natural for parents to want to be heroes in their children's lives. But, overindulgent parents achieve false-hero status by rescuing their children from the consequences they deserve.

2. Some parents want to keep their children as children, no matter how old they become. Many parents mourn every passage, as their children become adults. For example, when their toddlers are no longer toddlers, most parents mourn that they no longer have toddlers. When teenagers leave home, many parents suffer from Empty Nest Syndrome. Overindulgent parents suppress their feelings of loss by keeping their children over-dependent. As a result, their children never become independent and self-reliant. Instead, they cling to their parents even as adults.

What happens when parents buffer the blows of children's misbehavior?

Children, who are never guided or do not experience consequences for their misbehavior, lose the skills needed to manage life. Everyone's life eventually has complicated issues. Psychologically healthy adults gradually learned the skills to manage their life and its complications as they progressed from childhood, through adolescence, and into adulthood. Few overindulged children learn the self-management skills they need to manage their life.

To manage problems, parents need to teach children:

♦ to recognize that a problem exists.
♦ to consider their contribution to the problem.
♦ to fix the problem and make amends.

When overindulgent parents buffer their children, their coddled children do not gather the skills to manage life, including solving problems, getting along with others, being responsible and honest, and so much more. These are skills they will need as adults, when parents are no longer able to fix their children's problems.

I have noticed in my practice that children have three distinct reactions when overindulgent parents buffer them from the consequences of their misbehavior: dependency, a lack of age-appropriate skills, and an inflated self-image. These reactions perplex children. On the one hand, overindulgent parents inflate their children's self-image by talking about their positive qualities. On the other hand, these children have no skills, because their parents are doing everything for them.

This creates a Catch-22 dilemma. Overindulged and dependent children become resentful toward their parents, but they have no skills to achieve independence. Dependency and resentment continue to grow until there is an eventual breakdown in parent/child relationships. Often these dependent children stay dependent when they become adults. They also become emotionally distant with their parents. Why?

When a child misbehaves and a responsible parent disciplines that child, the parent teaches the child responsibility. Being responsible teaches children how to invest in others. Without responsibility, they do not know whom to invest in and they become emotionally distant.

Here is an example of a great mentoring parent who taught his son how to invest, through consequences:

A six-grade student carved his own name in his desk at school. The school principal wanted it replaced so he called the student's father. I happened to be working in the principals' office and heard the father whale through the phone, "I am not paying for anything and I will be right over there." I told the principal that either we are in trouble or the boy is!

What arrived at the principal's door was a man who was about 6' 4". He was dressed in overalls and very dusty from working in his shop. He pointed at both of us with a large finger and said, "You two come with me!" I did not argue with this man.

We went to the classroom and this father instructed his son to place the desk into the hallway. He directed his son to take all of his notebooks and books out of his desk. He told the teacher to have his son work on the floor until the desk was repaired. He made it very clear that he did not want his son to have another desk - he was to work on the floor.

After school he arrived with a toolbox. He said to his son, "I intentionally did not bring an electric-sander. I want you to sand the desk by hand." It took the student three days of sanding, two hours every day after school.

When the name was removed the father said, "That looks good, but we will never match the color of the rest of the desk. Sand the rest of the desk." He continued sanding for another three days. When this was finished the dad said, "I am going to show you how to stain your desk." Then his dad said to the teacher, "For the next three days he will varnish it, let it dry and steel wool it."

After ten days of working on the floor in class, he now had the most beautiful desk in his classroom. He would say to children, "Don't touch my desk. Stay away from my desk." He was proud of his desk!

Now that's a mentoring parent. He made his son invest both emotionally and physically through consequences for his misbehavior. He also taught his son a new skill.

Overindulgent Belief # 4: Sting-Free Discipline

Overindulgent parents either offer no discipline to children or take the sting out of their discipline.

Parents, who take the sting out of discipline, use a pop psychology idea that I believe can be a very sabotaging parenting tactic. Parenting experts often suggest that when children misbehave, parents should address their children's misbehavior, but separate the children from their behavior by refraining from criticizing them. So if Johnny lies, he is not a liar. Instead, Johnny is a good child who does bad lying behavior.

This parenting tactic is helpful for parents who verbally abuse their children. It forces parents to stop abusive labeling by focusing on children's behavior. But with most parents I believe this idea is sabotaging, because it takes the sting out of discipline. I am also concerned this parenting technique creates irresponsible children.

Often coupled with this idea is another saboteur: Parents who offer sting-free discipline do not apply labels to their children. They believe negative labels hurt their self-esteem. This is not true if the negative labels come with mentoring.

Here is the concern. When does a child who lies become a liar? When does a child who steals become a thief? This is confusing to children. Are they liars when they lie or nice children who lie a lot? Are they thieves when they steal or nice children who are fond of stealing? If a teenager came into your home and stole all of your cherished possessions, what would you call that teen: A nice teen that steals—or would you call that teen a thief? Most of us would call the intruder a thief.

For younger children, heavy labels are obviously harmful. Younger children do all kinds of mischief as they learn the rules of the world. Since younger children do not know the rules of the world yet, to label them would be unfair and possibly, self-fulfilling. But as children grow, they need to develop a sense of right and wrong, and recognize the impact of consequences. Labels help accomplish this.

Consider the issue of a person's reputation. Labels are useful in describing someone's reputation. For example, if people were to describe you, they would use labels to describe your reputation. Without labels, no one could describe you as having a good or bad reputation.

Reputation is important, and knowing a person's reputation is just as important. If I referred you to a counselor I described as warm-hearted, generous, disarming, gentle, competent, and dependable, consider your reaction to those labels. What if I described another counselor as threatening, irresponsible, ruthless, and greedy? Consider your ability to trust this counselor with your deepest concerns. Labels give you important information to help you make better decisions. When parents separate children from their behavior and refuse to use labels, they lose the emotional sting of their discipline.

Why does discipline need to have an emotional sting?

Many parenting experts define discipline as a learning experience. But, rarely do they discuss children feeling the emotional sting of discipline. Discipline needs to teach children how to behave, but children should also feel the emotional sting of discipline.

For example:

Bob's buddy is always disappointing Bob. His disappointment is an emotional sting—it hurts. His buddy says he is going to come to play with Bob, but often does not show up. He invites Bob to go to a show, but then goes with someone else, leaving Bob at home.

Every time his buddy lets him down, Bob feels the emotional sting of disappointment. This is teaching Bob an important lesson if he applies good thinking to the emotional sting of disappointment: "Never count on this buddy, because he is irresponsible." In fact, if Bob attached further good thinking to his disappointment, he may decide to find a more dependable friend.

❧

The same lesson is true when children feel the emotional sting of disappointment when they are disciplined. By using good thinking in conjunction with the emotional sting, discipline can motivate children to change.

Remember in Chapter One, the story about the underachieving boy whose parents overindulged him with a limousine ride for his graduation. They were covering-up his embarrassment by pretending that he performed well in school. Well, his parents took away his emotional sting. Instead of covering up his embarrassment, they should be honest with everyone so he would experience the emotional sting of embarrassment. When overindulgent parents take the emotional sting out of their children's discipline, they stop their children from learning important lessons.

Consider this parenting idea: I am going to give you one of the greatest secrets of influencing children when they misbehave. Here it is!

Predict for your children what will happen if they continue to misbehave, and use labels.

Parental prediction increases your influence with your children, especially as your children become teenagers. For example, if your child steals, you can predict that others will label your child as a thief. You can predict for your child that whenever anything is missing, others will accuse him or her of stealing. Then you can predict for your child that getting a reputation (as a thief) will complicate his or her life.

Of course, when your children refuse to listen, allow them to receive the full consequences of their misbehavior. Then, when your prediction comes true, whether your children admit it or not, they will realize that you are right. This will increase your influence with your children. With greater influence, you can guide your children to take better actions.

Why do parents take the sting out of their discipline?

1. Some parents want their children to consider them as "nice." Wanting a reputation of being a nice person, especially with children, is not a bad quality. But parenting is not a popularity contest! Sometimes it demands taking unpopular stances. There are times when parents need to be "not nice." Consider this example:

Teddy was failing at school, but he had mentoring parents. He wanted his parents to lie to his grandparents about his failing grades. When his parents refused to lie, he thought they betrayed him. Their truthfulness seemed like a "not nice" quality, but it was actually a necessary quality, because hiding his grades would misrepresent his poor scholastic achievements and shield him from feelings of embarrassment. When accompanied by good thinking, embarrassment is an emotional sting that can teach Teddy that he needs to be responsible and study more.

For many children, studying seems naturally painful. If parents focus on having a "nice" reputation with their children, they are more likely to let children off the hook when they refuse to study. There are times to be nice and there are times to be firm. Overindulgent parents believe that parenting is a popularity contest. Parenting is not a popularity contest, because there are times when you need to do some very unpopular parenting!

2. Overindulgent parents ignore their children's imperfections. For example, parents see their newborn babies as bundles of beautiful perfection. But I believe God turns babies into teenagers to keep parents humble. As their babies become teenagers, realistic parents change their view of their children to keep a realistic balance. This changing of their view is a natural part of parenting, because children need to express their God-given talents, which may not include parents' hopes and fantasies. Some parents, stuck in denial, strive to keep their fantasy children alive.

   Other parents believe if they give their children little or no discipline, their children will magically become the fantasy children they desire. These parents offer a passive parenting attitude, despite evidence that their children's misbehavior is getting progressively worse.

The major characteristic of parents, fixated on rearing fantasy children, is glorification of their children. As previously mentioned, their children may have the worst jobs in the world, but "glorified" parents believe their ideal children have the best jobs in the world. Their children could be driving a junk heap, but idol-making parents glorify it into the best car in the world. Although their children are not achieving the fantasy these parents hope for, glorifying parents ignore reality and preserve a fantasy that their hopes are coming true. As they continue to see their children as perfect, they see nothing to discipline. Without discipline, children receive no emotional sting and no mentoring. Self-guidance will not develop without the emotional sting of discipline. Without quality self-guidance, children are headed for behavior problems—and struggles throughout life.

Overindulgent Belief # 5: Highest Priority

Overindulgent parents believe their children are the highest priority in their family.

Overindulgent parents lift their children to the highest priority within their families. This is a major problem! Children should be a high priority in all families, but not the highest priority. The highest priority is reserved for the marital relationship, which is the epicenter of a family.

When one spouse views the other as the highest priority and the other spouse does the same, these couples rarely need marriage counseling! This healthy priority says to a spouse "I will always consider my spouse first in all my thoughts, decisions, and actions." With this shared priority, married couples are mindful of each other with mutual respect. However, if one spouse does not make their spouse the highest priority, marital problems ignite. When this happens, the neglected spouse yearns "My needs, my needs, my needs," because critical needs are not being met in the relationship.

When emotional needs are not met in their marriage, parents often turn to their children. This shift of priorities, from spouse to children, allows children to advance to the highest priority within their families. This creates critical dilemmas for children, because they are incapable of buffering their parents' marital problems.

Marital problems are not the only issues that allow children to advance to the highest priority in their families. Unfortunately, overindulgent parents misinterpret the concept of "child-centered" parenting, believing they should make their children the highest priority of their families. In reality, children do not have the intelligence to be the highest priority of their families. Parents are the only people in families capable enough to be in-charge of a household. So, when children become the most influential members of their families, under the guise of being the highest priority, families become complicated.

What happens when overindulgent parents make their children the highest priority of their families?

When children are the highest priority in their families, overindulgent parents shift decision-making responsibilities to their children, which allow children to take charge of their family. The chick is in charge of the henhouse! The tail is wagging the dog!

An example of children's power in "child-centered" families occurs when parents are willing to sacrifice finances and accumulate extreme credit card debt to give their children luxuries and fun activities. Someone may ask, "Isn't it noble for parents to sacrifice for their children?" It is, when children are in "harm's way" with a life threatening illness or dangerous life experience. In those situations, most parents appropriately make their children the highest priority and would sacrifice everything to save their children. But when parents put their credit rating and retirement in "harm's way" by buying another expensive toy or another fun activity—that is another matter.

Siblings contribute to this financial issue. Siblings are "fairness detectors" with a warped sense of fairness. Children constantly oversee their parents' fairness. With siblings, children monitor and enforce getting their fair share of stuff. Also, children tend to forget everything they get from their parents because they are focused on the "here and now."

When seven-year-old Michelle saw her parents buy her sister a new toy, Michelle did not think, "Yesterday my parents bought me a new toy, so now my sister and I are even. My parents sure are treating us fairly." Instead, Michelle focused on the "here and now" and complained, "Hey, that's not fair. If she is getting a new toy, I should get one too!" Parents, who make their children the highest priority, would accept Michelle's complaint as legitimate. Michelle convinces her parents, with her narrow definition of fairness, to buy her another toy. Michelle is now in-charge! With a child's mind, she becomes the power-center of her family. She decides how fairness works in her family and when her parents should buy her toys.

When parents embrace a child's immature thinking, the goals of the family shift. Michelle does not want to hear her parents explain that she got a gift yesterday, so she should not get a gift today. Her sister received a gift today, so Michelle wants a gift today.

Never become bound by a definition of fairness based on gifts and privileges. Always remember that true fairness gives equal love, not equal gifts. You can love your children equally, but you should raise them differently. Children have different personalities, different temperaments, different reactions to discipline, and countless other differences. Some children are easy and some are not. So, when a parent accepts a child's immature definition of fairness, suggesting that parents should act the same for each child, parents lose the empowerment to raise their children as individuals. When accepting their children's immature definition of fairness, parents dispense expensive rituals of "false-respect" onto their children.

For example:

I asked a recent high school graduate where she was going to college and she gleefully replied, "Denver, Colorado." Since this college was out-of-state with expensive tuition, I assumed that she was pursuing a specialized field of study. When I asked her what she was majoring in, she said, "I haven't decided yet." When I asked her why she was going to Colorado she replied, "It's pretty!" Why would her parents pay all that extra money for college, without a special purpose? The answer is—a false, but expensive, ritual of respect. She wants it, she gets it!

*What happens to children when they become the highest
priority of their families?*

The answer is that children attain power, too much
power! Power they are incapable of handling. Children need
their parents' guidance. When parents do not provide proper
guidance, children feel pressure (or permission) to take
charge of their families, striving to prove they are the most
powerful persons in their families.

Children need to know their limits. Without limits, they
pressure parents to yield to childish whims and fancies.
When parents offer few limits, children realize they are in-
charge. When they become teenagers without limits, they
believe they can do anything. When other authority figures
such as teachers, principals, and police officers impose limits with discipline, these teenagers feel no motivation to
change. Instead, they become oppositional. Teenagers without limits are like automobiles without steering wheels.
They could do anything. Anything!

Children, who are the highest priority in their families,
do not have the ability to uphold this lofty status. They lose
their childhood and they lose the safety of knowing their
parents are creating a healthy family with well-defined limits, a family that children can rely on.

Overindulgent Belief # 6: Wishy-Washy Decisions

*Overindulgent parents have difficulty making
firm decisions.*

Parenting experts suggest that parents gradually increase
negotiating with their children, as they become older. This is a
great idea. Parents need to replace control talk with influential

talk, as children become teenagers. Unfortunately, overindulgent parents negotiate every issue with their children, at all ages. Every topic is open for negotiation, even with young children. This creates children who act like attorneys, offering one-sided debates to get the best deal. This is a problem that intensifies, as children become teenagers!

When overindulgent parents waver in their decisions by over-negotiating with young children, children realize their parent's decisions are not final. All decisions are negotiable. This becomes a problem because parents and young children have two different goals when negotiating. When most parents negotiate, they are willing to compromise – meet in the middle. When young children negotiate, they want to win. Under these circumstances, parents can easily lose their influence.

Over-negotiation is an example of a parenting skill used at the wrong time. Parents, with good intentions, are negotiating with young children. This results in parents who become wishy-washy in their decision-making. Unlike young children, many older children understand that negotiation can result in mutual compromise. So, negotiation often works well when parents negotiate with more mature children, but not with younger children.

Why do parents have difficulty making firm decisions?

1. Some parents dislike decision-making and shift it onto others, so they can avoid the responsibility that comes with decision-making. At work, they shift decision-making onto fellow employees. In their personal life, they shift decision-making onto their friends. In marriage, they shift their decision-making onto their spouses. In parenting, they shift their decision-making onto their children.

2. Some parents shift decision-making onto children, believing children should have equal status with adults in their family. Children do have equal status, but they do not have equal brainpower. Overindulgent parents give children too much decision-making power, believing they are building children's self-esteem. In reality, when children make decisions before they are capable, they are set up to fail, which damages their self-esteem.

What happens to children with parents who do not make firm decisions?

Dr. B. C. Nelms in "Attachment vs. Spoiling" in 1983 found that ambivalent and confused parents could not define the difference between nurturing behavior and overindulgence. This creates parents who waver and become "wishy-washy" with their decisions. Parents, who make wishy-washy decisions, have children who are always trying to discover their limits. When everything is negotiable, there are no limits. Children constantly question and push on how far they can go with their behavior.

When children are asked to prematurely make decisions, their decisions are usually bad. Many children, forced into adult decisions, either become self-inflated or insecure. As adults, they often view decision-making as a pressure-filled responsibility they would rather avoid. This promotes over-dependence on others to make decisions for them. This results in children losing the essential life-management skill of making good decisions.

Overindulgent Belief # 7: Too Trusting

Overindulgent parents are too trusting.

When parents feel inadequate about their parenting skills, guilt is often the result. The combination of inadequacy and guilt creates parents who are susceptible to their children's guilt trips. To erase their guilt, parents become too trusting of their children. They believe that if they trust their children more, they will solve two problems. They will feel less guilt and their children will be happy.

Parents want to believe their children, but children are children and they occasionally misbehave. For example, when children occasionally lie they may use manipulative guilt, suggesting to their parents, "If you were a good parent, you would believe me."

When overly-trusting parents feel guilt, they edit facts so they can continue to believe their children. If other authorities, such as teachers, principals, or counselors, tell parents the truth about their children, overly-trusting parents disregard the advice and support of those authorities.

Why are overindulgent parents too trusting? Why do they edit reality, when they hear facts about their children from other authority figures?

1. Some parents are too trusting because they equate trust with being good parents. To maintain the image of a good parent they decide, "My children are right and everyone else is wrong." This belief leads to complications because it affects others. Consider this very serious example:

   A couple arranged counseling for their teenage daughter with me. She vandalized their neighbor's house. When I was taking a history of the girl's back-ground, I asked the standard questions about drug use. I had her tested and found that she had cocaine and heroin in her system during the time of the van-dalism. When I asked her parents about their concerns with the test results, they immediately defended their daughter and assured me she was only experimenting with drugs. I told them that I defined drug experimentation as the occasional use of mari-juana, and that using cocaine and heroin was far from experimentation. Her parents became angry and viewed me as a monster, because I would not edit reality. I became the "bad" psychologist because I would not leave reality behind.

When parents inappropriately attack others to mini-mize their children's serious misbehavior, they stop dealing with the reality of their children's very serious misbehavior.

2. Parents, who trust too much, often want to be rescuers for their children. By being rescuers, parents see them-selves as good parents in an evil world. They see their children as victims and they readily believe any stories about their children's victim status. This is especially true of parents who harbor anger. Angry parents easily ally with their upset children. This allows angry parents to unleash their long-standing anger at targets. Instead of properly managing their anger, they unleash anger at anyone who criticizes their children—even those who have legitimate concerns.

When angry parents unleash their anger at others, they believe they are bonding with their children. They are actually creating a dysfunctional alliance. Alliances are not bonds. Alliances are temporary agreements to fend off, attack or blame others. Unlike alliances, bonds are deep and permanent relationships based on truth. Alliances easily shift and break. Bonds are much stronger because they are grounded on truthful acceptance of children, including their flaws.

Continuing with the example of drug abuse, if one parent changes his or her thinking and accepts the drug problem with their daughter, the other parent is in a bind. If they have an alliance, it would not be safe for either of them to consider the possibility of drug abuse with their daughter, because the "aware" parent becomes the bad-guy in the eyes of the denial parent. When this occurs, conflict often arises with the goal of getting the "aware" parent to get back into an alliance by avoiding the reality of the drug abuse

If parents are too trusting to accept the real flaws of children, they stop children from making important changes.

Overindulgent Belief # 8: "I Will Correct My Parents' Mistakes"

Overindulgent parents believe their parents raised them improperly. It is the longing of overindulgent parents to correct their own parents' mistakes, by becoming perfect parents.

Parents using this overindulgent belief often share this parenting creed: "I shall repair my childhood by replaying my childhood through my children. I shall be a 'child-centered' parent and give my children everything they want to ensure their happiness. I shall be the perfect parent my parents never were. If I do this, I shall be a good parent. We will bond and my children will be happy."

When parents practice this parenting creed, their sole purpose is to erase their own parents' mistakes. They do this by preserving the illusion that they will make their children happy by being better parents than the parents who raised them. Instead, these parents create a new set of mistakes. They raise their children based on parenting they wanted from their own parents, which stops them from realizing the "actual" parenting needs of their own children.

Why is each generation of parents convinced the previous generation did such a bad job of parenting? If the previous generation of parents did such a bad job of parenting, how did this current generation of adults become one of the most advanced in technology, information, education, and enlightenment?

Is your childhood important? Yes, but the past is no more important than the present and the future. The past cannot change, so true empowerment (which is the bedrock of counseling) is in the present, which affects the future.

Why is it important to review the past?

The past is only part of a large puzzle. It is important to know the impact of the past, but realizing the impact must serve a useful, not destructive, purpose. Sometimes adults obsess about the past, especially if they had a difficult childhood. Adults can stop obsessing about the past by considering all three parts of life (past, present, and future). Consider this empowerment question: If you had a difficult childhood, what are you going to do about it now?

Why do parents, hurt during their childhood, blame their parents for their own lack of parenting skills? I am going to give you my favorite answer: "I don't know." A more productive path, when adults review their childhood, is to create a change that improves their present life and their future.

Most adults had a combination of good and bad experiences when growing up, with parents giving loving support, as well as emotional pain. A healthy goal for parents is to understand the strengths and flaws of their own parents.

Parents need to embrace the positive qualities of their own parents and actively improve any negative influences. When parents feel true emotional pain about their childhood, they need to avoid the blame game. Here is a better alternative. Parents can view their own parents as real people with strengths and flaws. This gives parents empowerment, not by angrily obsessing about the past, but by focusing on the present and the future, where empowerment and change reside.

If you want to review your own parents' influence on you, try it with a healthy attitude. For example, my father was like any other person with strengths and flaws. When I reviewed my childhood, instead of criticizing my father for his flaws, I searched for what he directly and indirectly taught me. I also seek to use these lessons today.

What my father taught me, and how I use it today:

1. My father taught me that time spent with children is important. He taught me this, not because he was there much, as he was a typical 1950s–1960s father. He worked hard. I now understand his work ethic. I also understand the impact of his limited time at home. This motivates me to spend considerable time with my children.

2. He told colorful stories about the personalities of family members of previous generations, which made me feel connected to them. He was good at this! I am too!

3. He taught me that education is important. He had none and he shared how it affected him through his frustrations and wishes for careers he never attained. This is one of the greatest lessons he taught me.

4. He taught me not to give up on my dreams, because he often did. You are reading my second book: another dream came true!

5. He taught me to hate 9-to-5 jobs, because he hated his for thirty years.

6. He taught me how important religion was to him by his reluctance to express his religious beliefs, for fear of embarrassment. His embarrassment to speak about religion was as strong as his beliefs. I am not afraid to express my religious beliefs.

7. He was an honest person. He taught me to tell the truth and he physically disciplined me when I was dishonest. He was not abusive when he spanked. I earned it and I knew it. I also value telling the truth.

8. He used body language to show love, because he had difficulty saying, "I love you." He taught me to say, "I love you" because he had difficulty saying, "I love you."

9. He taught me to buy a car by not giving me one. Self-reliance is a blessing in any era, especially today.

10. When he died, he taught me there is a limit to a life span. I try to use it well.

I could view my father as a neglectful workaholic. I have chosen the mindset that I want to learn from his strengths and flaws. If I believed my father should have been perfect, then he came up short. The mindset I choose is to see him as a human father of the 1950s-1960s who did what his times expected. A man I can learn from to change my present and future life for the better. From his strengths and flaws, I learned lessons that helped me set my priorities. Therefore, the mindset I have chosen allows me to feel great love for him. Even though he has been dead for years, "Dear Old Dad" is still doing good work today. Thanks Dad!

I regularly advise parents not to worry about passing the bad affects of their own parents on to their children. All parents will have their own unique affects on their children, good and bad. It is helpful if you have this "learning mindset" when you review your childhood.

Overindulgent Belief # 9: "Who Am I And Why Am I Here?"

Overindulgent parents need more identity development, which means they do not know who they are or why they are here.

Overindulgent parents need to create their own identities because:

1. Some parents limit their identities to their careers, which are demanding and lessen the time to be active in other parts of their lives, such as parenting.

2. Other parents define their identities only by their children's current level of happiness.

People need a thorough understanding of themselves well before they become parents. Their decision to become parents should be based on their identity. Identity is a truthful understanding of oneself. So, identity requires:

+ realizing your personal strengths and weaknesses;
+ having values reflecting decency that are consistent;
+ living life to its fullest, with a purpose.

These are requirements that many adults avoid by ignoring personal strengths and weaknesses, having inconsistent values, and not having a purpose in life.

Another requirement for identity is a foundation of core beliefs. The best way to discover if you have core beliefs is to consider your opinions about hot controversial topics such as abortion, right to die, or belief in God. If you do have opinions about these issues, great! You have an identity, because you have thought about the important issues of life. If you do not have strong opinions about hot controversial topics, then your identity needs enhancing. When asked about hot controversial topics, adults without firm identities agree with whoever is dominating the conversation. Parents, without identities, struggle when helping children create identities for several reasons:

+ Children model their parents and if parents have little identity to model, children lose an important resource for the creation of their own identity.
+ Some parents do not realize that they exist for a purpose. Having a purpose creates a life with direction. Without direction, it is difficult for parents to guide children.
+ Other parents have a dream about what they want to be, but did not reach it. They never modify their dreams to make them more attainable, so they give up.

Pete was a father who always wanted to be a football player in high school and college. He was big enough and he had a thorough understanding of football strategies. But he was clumsy. He never reached his desire to be a football player, but he loved the game. As an adult, he found himself stuck in a job that did not resemble his interest in football or any other interest.

His son was big and ready for football. Pete was happy to be involved in football again, and his son delighted in receiving Pete's attention. Together they practiced football and prepared for tryouts. As they worked together, Pete saw the same irritating clumsiness within his son. He tried to help his son correct these problems, but became more irritated with each failure.

Once when Pete was helping his son practice, his son's clumsiness was unbearable. Pete suddenly became frustrated and violent, pushing his son against their house. He was about to punch his son when his wife intervened. This violent reaction baffled everyone, including Pete, because Pete was not a violent man.

Pete's passion remained with football, although his career went elsewhere. When he saw an opportunity to regain his identity (vicariously through his son), Pete was thrilled. But when he saw the same frustrating clumsiness emerge from his son, Pete popped a cork. He released his frustrations on his son when he was reminded of his own flaws.

When Pete entered counseling, I helped him realize he needed to take action. He was in a career that did not reflect his true identity, which made him feel empty - passionless. Through counseling, he learned that football was a major part of his identity. He knew he had a brain for football. He knew football strategies better than most football coaches.

In one counseling session, he gained an insight. He complained that it would take him four years to finish a degree to become a football coach. He sadly said he would be 48 years old, suggesting that it was too late. I advised Pete that he could become 48 years old and happy, or he could become 48 years old and miserable. Either way, Pete was going to be 48 years old.

Pete went back to school. He is now a high school coach living a dream, instead of bitterly dreaming about life. He loves molding teenagers into adults with his love of football. He is teaching his students about life through football. He has a purpose in life!

Why would people not want to create their own identity?

1. Creating an identity is pleasurable, painful, and requires taking risk in life. Many people appreciate the pleasurable part, but do not care for pain and risk-taking. Both are necessary, but uncomfortable. Risk-taking increases a person's opportunity for success and failure. Many people want to avoid the painful failure of risk-taking, but it is from failures that people learn how to succeed.

   Successful parents have a survival skill that I consider to be one of their greatest assets. When successful parents fail, the first thought they have after experiencing failure is "Okay, it does not work this way. How am I going to make it work? What are my choices?"

   I counseled Pete to incorporate this survival skill into his thinking. He wanted to be in football, but he believed he should have been a football player and missed his chance. When he assessed his skills by considering his past, present, and future, he learned to adapt his dream. He realized that he had all the necessary skills to be a great football coach. He learned that if he wanted to enjoy life, he needed to take a bold risk (go back to school to change his career).

He found making changes a bit scary and required a sacrifice of time, money, and effort. It is a rare person who has an incredibly happy and successful life by chance. But, many people sit back and wait to be happy. Pete invested in his life, and is now looking forward to his future.

I often ask parents, "If you were Pete's son, which parent would you rather have as a model to guide your life? Would you prefer a parent who unleashes frustrated anger at you, or would you prefer a parent who knows what he wants and goes after it? Which parent would be a more attractive leader? Which parent would be easier for children to bond?"

2. Another quality, of people with identities, is that they know their values. Values include honesty, loyalty, and consistency. Parents without firm identities have inconsistent values, which creates confused children. For example, what messages do parents send when they reprimand a child for stealing, but then cheat on their taxes? What if grandfather is dead, but a child hears that grandfather is sleeping? In both cases, parents have damaged the value of honesty. Values, such as honesty, offer a foundation leading parents to create consistency, stability, and predictability in their emotions, thoughts, actions, and relationships.

Let's consider values for a moment. There are essentially two types of values: basic values and selected values. Basic values teach children about their conscience. So, without basic values children become bad people.

People select all of their values, but basic values are necessary for everyone. For example, safety is a basic value and vital for quality relationships. When people are together, they assume they will be safe with one another. But what if the basic value of safety does not exist within a family? Without safety, close personal relationships fray and deteriorate. In an era of "Don't tell me what my values are," basic values are becoming more essential than ever before. When people do not have basic values, they do bad things and become bad people.

So, basic values create a foundation in parent-child relationships. The basic values of safety, honesty and consistency create parents that children can rely on.

Selected values are values that people select with their own priorities. For example, when considering a hot controversial topic such as abortion, one person may prioritize the value of personal freedom and be pro-choice. Another person may prioritize the value of life and be pro-life. Both are people with selected values, but they have different selected values.

If these two people have the same basic values (safety, honesty, integrity), but different selected values (Pro Choice vs. Pro Life), they can respect one other's views without hostility. If they do not have basic values, they become hostile and may harm each other.

Family members can have different "selected" values and continue to be respectful if they have basic values. If family members do not share "basic" values, the family is in serious jeopardy. When parents do not have "basic" values, serious harm can come to children.

Summary

This chapter taught you the beliefs of overindulgent parents. If you have any of these beliefs, with good intentions, you may be driving a wedge between you and your children. But, knowing about the overindulgent beliefs is the first step to making changes. The next step is to learn to think like a mentoring parent. You will enjoy the next chapter, which is designed to give you a new way of thinking as a parent.

~ CHAPTER 3 ~

How to Think Like a Mentoring Parent

The goal of this chapter is to help you think like a mentoring parent. Many parenting techniques do not work because they attempt to change parents' behavior (how they react to children), but not their overall thinking. To mentor, you need to think like a mentor. After you learn to think like a mentor, then we will discuss parenting techniques.

The foremost goals of overindulgent parents are to be a buddy to their children and to make their children happy. The foremost goal of mentoring parents is to give their children game-plans to manage all parts of life, so children feel confident within themselves.

The thinking-qualities of the mentoring parent help solidify your family, while at the same time teach your children to be self-reliant. Use the qualities of the mentoring parent to replace overindulgence and you will become your children's parent, a mentoring parent.

Becoming a mentoring parent requires that you change your understanding of your job as a parent and your purpose in raising children. Your purpose as a parent is to mentor your children with the goal of raising self-reliant children.

Warning! Your children will initially resist your new style of parenting. Your children will want their overly permissive parents to go back to their old overindulgent ways. But if you persist, you will have a wonderful result—a real bond with your children!

The principles of the mentoring parent are not a parenting theory. Instead, they give you a usable and dynamic style of parenting which is easy to put into practice. As you learn the qualities of a mentoring parent, you will shed the role of "buddy" and become a real parent to your children.

In my counseling practice, I have witnessed a shift of family power from parents to children, which devastates families. The principles, you are about to learn, will put order back into your family. You are about to learn how to think as a mentoring parent.

Quality #1: "I Will Raise My Children"

Mentoring parents believe that they should raise their children. They do not abdicate their childrearing responsibilities to others.

To mentor children, parents need to be available to their children. They need to be at home. I want to emphasize emphatically that this is not a political statement to keep mothers at home. This is not a gender issue. It does not matter which parent stays home; the priority is that at least one parent spends considerable time at home, mentoring children. It is just a fact that mentoring parents cannot mentor to their children if they are not with their children.

Georgia and Bart were unhappy with the results of their parenting. Their daughter was in a quality day-

care center. Both Georgia and Bart worked 40-plus hours a week outside their home. In spite of her quality daycare center, their daughter was not bonding with them as much as they hoped.

I asked them to do an experiment, (which you can do as well). I asked them to sit on their front porch and watch neighborhood children coming home from school. I asked them to determine which neighborhood children were heading home to a parent and which were going to an empty house. Georgia and Bart easily recognized the difference. The children going home to an empty house seemed unhappy, out-of-control, or both.

This experiment was a life-changing event for Georgia and Bart. Previously, they mentored their daughter when it was convenient for them. The problem is, children need mentoring all of the time. Watching their unhappy neighborhood children convinced Georgia and Bart they needed to get serious about their mentoring.

This example illustrates a major problem that all working parents experience. Issues arise throughout each day where children need advice, moral training, emotional support, hugs, appraisal, encouragement, and much more. No nanny, daycare worker, or babysitter can give the special connection that exists between you and your children.

Consider this: What would happen if you hired a consultant to help you with computer problems, but the consultant was never available when you needed help? If you had to get someone else to manage the computer problem, your consultant is useless. The same is true of parenting. There is no substitute for you!

The Priority of Children:

It is only possible to be a mentoring parent if you spend notable time with your children. While most mentoring can wait until you come home from work, some mentoring issues cannot wait. Children have daily emotional and moral issues that need immediate attention. Overindulgent parents rationalize their lack of involvement by quick-fixing their neglect with a cycle of overindulgence.

Instead of giving children a mentoring parent, overindulgent parents evaluate their parenting with a "marketing" definition of happiness. Our culture has marketed the idea that children can be happy with more materialism and more freedoms. This marketing definition of happiness leads overindulgent parents to believe they only need to buy another toy or say "yes" to another freedom—freedoms that children are not prepared to manage.

Wendy, the rationalizer, was a parent who wanted everything in life. She had a beautiful career and a wonderful nanny who attended to her daughter's needs. As her daughter progressed through high school and college, Wendy felt a growing emotional distance with her daughter. During all of those potentially bonding years, Wendy's daughter had everything except a mentoring parent.

Fortunately—or unfortunately—Wendy hired a nanny, who created a beautiful bond with her daughter, but Wendy never did bond with her child—she was too busy. She rationalized that if her daughter was at home with a wonderful nanny, her daughter was happy. The wall between Wendy and her daughter grew.

This is very sad because Wendy didn't get a real relationship when her daughter became an adult. As her daughter became an adult, Wendy regretted the tremendous distance and strain she felt with her daughter.

To have a nice home for their children, many parents rationalize that both parents need to work. Many parents believe that a nice home must be an expensive home. Small and cozy is not the norm in today's housing market. In the 1950s, the average size home was roughly 1,200 square feet. Today the average size home is 2,800 square feet. It is ironic that so many parents assume incredible debt to provide a nice home for children. They work long hours for that nice home and are rarely at home. This cycle perpetuates itself, creating more distance between parents and their children.

Of course, the home is not the real issue, as the debt becomes overwhelming for many families. Many families have what I call *False Wealth Syndrome*, as they are living above their financial means. They have so much "stuff" they appear wealthy, but they are actually drowning in debt. Their overwhelming debt becomes the main focus of these overworked and worried parents, who lose precious time to mentor to their children.

One real concern is that some families do not have two parents. For example, if one parent is dead, the surviving parent may be too busy to be a mentoring parent. Another reason is divorce. Parents, who have one income, have to prioritize work so they can survive. Although this is justifiable, parent mentoring often does not happen and this has a bad impact.

Whether it is divorce, abandonment, super-career parents, or *False Wealth Syndrome,* guilt is often the motivating emotion that nudges parents. Guilt pressures parents to acquire immediate remedies to promote their children's happiness, which leads many parents to use the quick-fix "marketing" definition of happiness—overindulgence.

Insights for the Mentoring Parents

Parent mentoring is a full-time job. Your first step as a mentoring parent is to attain more time with your children. Consider these next suggestions carefully and how you would adapt these ideas. Here are two questions to help you consider the relationship between your work and your parenting:

1. Which parent, you or your spouse, should do most of the mentoring?

   In any family, deciding which parent should mentor is not a gender issue. It is an issue of parenting skills. In other words, which parent (you or your spouse) is the best fit for your children as they grow? Which parent is less likely to overindulge your children? It may be that you are a better fit during certain times of your children's life, while your spouse is best at another time.

   Misty and Mark raised two boys, and Misty was the obvious parent of choice when their children were young. She was caring and nurturing, offering their children a strong base of security. As their two boys entered middle school, new influences affected their children, requiring a different set of skills which Misty did not have: firmness, boundaries, and tough-love. Misty and Mark switched roles, with Misty re-igniting her career and Mark staying home as the mentoring parent.

   This was a tough decision for Misty and Mark. These decisions are not always in the best financial interest of the family. Before they had children, they decided to live a lifestyle that gave them the time needed to mentor to their children. Their decision gave Misty and Mark excellent results.

2. Can mentoring parents earn an income and advance their careers while they parent?

Yes! It is possible, but it requires careful planning. Here are several questions that mentoring parents can ask themselves to evaluate their options:

+ Can one or both of you earn an income at home?
+ Does one of you have the skills to work where your children attend school (for example: secretary, teacher's aid, coach, attendance office, cafeteria, teacher)?
+ Can one of you work only when children are attending school?
+ Can either of you do e-commerce in their chosen field of work?
+ Does one parent earn enough money so the other parent can stay home?
+ Did you create huge and wasteful debt with a large house payment? Can you reduce your debt?

Many overindulgent parents have serious debt issues, which consumes their money and forces them to spend more time away from home. Consider Alicia and Philip.

Alicia and Philip lived in a large expensive home with all the amenities. They also had every toy, including a boat, camper, recreational vehicles, and more. But what they had most was crippling credit card debt.

Their two younger children were farmed out to expensive daycare centers, and their teenagers came home to an empty house. They believed they needed to have this large home to generate happiness within

*their children. They loved their home, so my sugges-
tion was difficult for them. I suggested they downsize!
It was a difficult decision, but they decided to get a
smaller home, sell some of their expensive toys, and
have a huge garage sale.*

*One evening when Philip came home from work to
their downsized home, Alicia was sitting in the middle
of the living room with all their children, plus six of
their children's friends. They were eating popcorn
and watching a movie. Both realized they had not had
the time to do this in their large home because they
were too busy paying for it*

There is no substitute for involved parents. Only you
can offer a healing hug to your children and mentor in your
own special way. Quality time spent with your children is
your best investment.

Just as an aside, I think big gorgeous homes are great –
if you can afford them. If you have a big home, consider
how you would increase the "gathering potential" of your
home.

For example, many homes have three to four televisions. If you have more than one television in your home,
you have decreased the "gathering potential" of your home.
When children come home and do not like what their parents are watching, they separate, heading for another
television. To increase the gathering potential of your home
put only one television in your home.

The same suggestion is true for computers and the
Internet. Never put a computer, computer game systems or
the Internet in your children's bedrooms. This increases
cocooning behavior! Your children will cocoon in their bedrooms and your gathering potential is destroyed. Also, if

you put the Internet in your children's bedroom, you put a perpetrator in the bedroom. Listen to this true story.

A radio personality had two policemen on his show. The policemen were experts in Internet and crime. They asked the radio personality to pick a chat-line for teens. The police presented themselves as a 14-year-old girl on the chat-line. In ten minutes they had 50 hits from men between the ages of 35 to 50 making sexual comments. The police said this response is very typical.

There is another special problem. The safest place in most children's lives is their bedroom. Sitting in their bedrooms, children are surrounded by the signals of safety. They apply these safe feelings to their conversations with perpetrators coming into their bedrooms through the Internet.

My best and safest suggestion, to you as a fellow parent, is to have one computer and one television in the family room. Never let your children isolate with the Internet.

Quality #2: The Whole Truth And Nothing But the Truth!

Mentoring parents have a deep commitment to truth and reality and help their children accept the joyful and painful parts of life.

Truth is one of the key foundations within a family. Without truth, families crumble. Mentoring parents have a deep commitment to truth. Mentoring parents believe their children need to be able to rely on their parents to always tell them the truth.

Miriam and Jack did not have the heart to tell their seven-year-old son the family dog was hit by a car and killed. So, they let their son believe the dog was missing, but still alive. They hoped to protect their son from the pain of grief, but every night their son would ask them to look for the dog.

These protective parents kept their secret and pretended to search for their dead dog. Eventually, in tears, he announced that the dog left because the dog did not like him. His parents' dishonesty led their son to this distorted belief. They unintentionally became co-conspirators in hurting their son.

Mentoring parents work hard to stop children's distorted thoughts and to manage emotions by telling the truth. When parents are not truthful, one lie creates a need for another lie and another. Children need to know that they can trust their parents to tell the truth. The best way to stop children's distorted thinking is to always tell your children the straight story.

When you talk to your children, there are two types of messages that they receive: a content message and a hidden message. When parents are truthful about an important issue, the content message honestly tells children what occurred. The hidden message, of offering the truth to children, is the message that you and your children can work together to manage difficult issues. Children also learn that if they ever need a straight story, they can count on you.

Truth is also important when discussing children's misbehavior. Mentoring parents believe that children need to hear the truth about their good behavior, as well as their misbehavior and limitations. They offer feedback to children in a caring and genuine manner. If parents give children inaccurate and dishonest feedback, they set up their children for problems.

*Tony's parents often told Tony, "You are gifted."
Since Tony was young, his dad spent enormous time*

with Tony, which sounds like a great investment. But Tony's dad was trying to mold Tony into something he was not. He wanted a gifted child and worked toward that goal since Tony was an infant. Tony came to believe in his giftedness. In reality, Tony had average intelligence and attended a school, which eventually recognized his average intelligence.

Tony had a difficult time adjusting to school. Since his father did not give him an accurate reflection of his skills and abilities, Tony had to deal with a distorted image in a public arena (his school), which complicated his life.

Mentoring parents never exaggerate their children's strengths or ignore their children's limits. Your children need to know that they can always count on you to give them truthful information, in a direct but caring manner. Anything less is a recipe for failure! Tony needs a mentoring parent who accepts him as he is and helps him progress as far as he can go. Many average children become exceptional adults if they are taught to honestly understand themselves.

Overindulgent parents glorify their children and ignore their flaws. This stops parents from becoming mentors. Without mentoring, parents and children do not bond. When parents accept their children, an authentic connection happens between parents and children. Truthfully tell your children about their strengths and their flaws.

Here is another consideration about truth. Mentoring parents never keep secrets, because secrets destroy family relationships. It is amazing how children learn about family secrets. They are little "truth detectors"— sponges absorbing every conversation not meant for them. They overhear telephone conversations or siblings and cousins tell them the rest of the story. They notice subtle changes in their parents when certain topics arise.

When children realize their parents keep secrets, their distrust brews. They wonder what other secrets exist. When secretive parents finally discuss family issues, children wonder if they are hearing a full story. When parents keep secrets, it forces them to deceive their children, which stops honest and wholesome family bonding. Mentoring parents do not keep secrets, and discuss all sensitive issues.

The problem with dishonesty and secrets is that both require continued lying. Liars forget and become inconsistent. So, it is important that parents tell their children the truth. Mentoring parents know that truthfulness creates consistency, because truth reflects reality. Lies become obvious over time. Your children need dependable, consistent and honest parents. Strive to be consistent and truthful, even with difficult issues.

Rationalizations For Not Being Truthful with Children:

One rationalization overindulgent parents believe is that a lie will protect their children from emotional pain. In the previous example with the missing dead dog, the boy eventually heard from a friend that his dog was dead and that his parents knew the dog was dead. His parents were unaware he learned the truth about his dog, and a deceptive wedge of dishonesty came between these parents and their child. His parents continued their deception, but their son recognized their deceptiveness. To retaliate, every night this boy would ask his parents to help him look for his dog, wondering when they would stop their charade. Instead of being protected from a painful experience, this boy was learning the art of manipulation and retaliation.

I often ask this question of parents who lie to protect their children: "Would you go to someone for support, knowing they are dishonest with you?" The answer most parents give is, "Of course not. When we have concerns, we go to people who are honest with us." Your children need your commitment to honesty.

Another concern is that when children become teenagers, their issues become more complicated. If you are honest with your young children, you will retain your influence when your children become teenagers.

Some parents think their children are deaf!

Recently, a parent told me a family secret, with his five-year-old child playing with a toy, sitting before us. I said to the parent, "I think he knows." The parent replied, "Ah, he did not hear that." To prove my suspicion, with the parent's permission I asked the child, "Do you know?" The child explained the secret in his five-year-old language. They have ears like sponges!

Insights for the Mentoring Parent:

Always be honest with your children. Your honesty creates the foundation for your entire family. Sometimes it is easy to be honest and other times it is difficult.

A media therapist was asked by a concerned parent, "Grandpa shot himself. What should we tell our six-year-old son?" Routinely the media therapist suggests that parents lie to their children and tell them it was an accident. But, every cousin knows the truth, every uncle and aunt knows the truth, and most family friends (young and old) know the truth. What a set-up! No parents can control all of those conversations.

I don't want to tell a six-year-old child that Grandpa shot himself, but if that is the truth it needs to be said. Of course, there is a need for many other conversations about this issue as this child grows and has different thoughts about Grandpa's death. But, if his parents tell this boy the truth, he knows that he can always get a straight story from his parents. That is the important lesson. Also, if his parents tell him the truth, they are all on the same playing-field as they make their adjustment together.

When you are honest with your children it enforces your family to deal with sensitive emotional issues, which creates much greater bonds.

Quality #3: Be All That You Can Be!

Mentoring parents think it is important that their children acquire their unique talents.

Mentoring parents strive to help their children acquire three sets of skills that lead to their unique talents. As we discuss these skills, consider how well your children are performing in each area.

1. *Dependency:* Dependency is a vital skill and needs to be used occasionally and temporarily. Dependency means your children will occasionally rely on another person for support.

   For example, if your children learn a musical instrument, such as a guitar, they will be dependent or rely on their teacher. Eventually they learn to play well and do not need their teacher. Or if your children are missing friends who moved away, it is appropriate for them to be temporarily dependent on you. They often cling and become dependent as they recover from losses. They gradually stop being dependent and return to their normal life, especially as they meet new friends. In other words, they retake the reigns of their lives.

Over-dependency becomes a problem when children get stuck on dependency and refuse to retake the reigns of their life. Over-dependent children stop their natural exploration of the world, which stops children from acquiring their skills, talents and self-reliance.

So, children need to know when to be dependent and when to stop being dependent. This starts very young in life. Many children cry at night in their bedrooms because they do not want to be left alone. They want to get into their parents' bedroom and be dependent on their parents to feel safe. Most mentoring parents realize that their children will need to cry and eventually the crying stops, as children adjust to staying in their bedrooms. This teaches children that they can feel safe within themselves.

2. *Mutual relationships:* Another important skill that your children should learn as they become adults is mutual relationships. Mutual relationships occur when sharing, concern, and agreement between people happens. For example, when spouses negotiate with each other before making decisions, a solid mutual relationship develops. Mutual relationships occur in classrooms when children take turns, stand in-line together, and help one another with assignments. Mutual relationships help affiliations thrive and grow. When children feel confident with the skills to manage relationships, it is easier for them to acquire their special skills and talents. They become more receptive to others and the knowledge others offer.

3. *Self-Reliance:* Self-reliance is having confidence in one's own judgment and acting on that judgment. There are times in your life when you've got to handle a problem yourself. Children are no different. They

need confidence to be self-reliant, so they can eventually handle any circumstance. One of the greatest sources of learning to be self-reliant is mentoring parents. When children observe their parents managing life, they learn to manage life.

Here is a huge problem with overindulgence. Most overindulgent children become over-dependent and unable to have mutual relationships and self-reliance. In other words, they know how to get parents to give them what they want, but they do not know how to share, show concern, or reach agreement with others. Nor do they learn how to stand on their own two feet. Without these skills, they cannot gain their unique talents or manage the complexities of life, because they are caught in the cycle of over-dependency.

Mentoring parents teach their children how to be dependent, interdependent, and self-reliant. Consider these further thoughts about these three sets of skills:

Dependency

Children instinctively cling to their parents when a sad event occurs or when they feel insecure. Mentoring parents help children become confident by facing the truth of the sad event, experiencing the sad emotions, and discussing the sad event together. If children have a flaw, parents honestly tell their children that they need to work on their flaw. Learning how to manage flaws creates confidence in children.

Overindulgent parents only offer children overindulgence, with the belief the overindulgence will magically erase their children's unhappiness and instill confidence. Unfortunately, overindulged children become over-dependent and expect their parents to continually fix their problems with more overindulgence.

Mutual Relationship

Your children need you to tell them how their behavior (especially misbehavior) effects others. You have probably seen your children do hurtful behavior that may have shocked you. You may have been more surprised that they did not have a clue about their effect on others. This is normal.

Mentoring parents tell children how their behavior affects others, which teaches them to show concern for others. This leads children to work well at school and in relationships. They take their turn, are less likely to interrupt, and have a sense of fairness for themselves and others.

Overindulgent parents teach their children to focus on themselves, which leads children to believe they require special treatment from everyone. This causes overindulgent children to become demanding and obnoxious. They learn to think of themselves only, and have little concern for others.

Always tell your children their positive and negative effects on other people. One of the greatest ways to promote understanding of their effect on others is to have them make amends. Making amends helps children connect with others and helps them consider how they impact others as well.

Early one morning, I was sitting in my living room. I happened to glance out the window and stopped. I spotted two children sneaking around the bushes on my neighbor's yard. They were laughing and pointing at my neighbor's car. Later my neighbor told me that someone had "egged" his car. I told him I knew the culprits. He talked with the culprits' fathers. One father said, "Boys will be boys" and did nothing. The other father enforced his mentoring. His son washed and waxed the egged car. Then he instructed his son to wash down the neighbor's driveway. Then he directed his son to work for the neighbor for the week-

end, which included cutting grass, washing windows and other odd jobs.

It is easy to see which father taught his son about mutual relationships and concern for others.

Self-Reliance

Children need to become self-reliant. For example, you can help your children study for a test, but at some point your children have to take the test by themselves. Parents can advise a teenager on handling a conflict with another teenager, but at some point the teenager needs to manage the conflict on his or her own. Mentoring parents explore options with their children, so their children gain confidence by realizing better choices and taking the reigns of their lives.

Self-reliance also includes children learning about and pursuing their dreams in life. Some overindulgent parents force their unmet dreams onto their children. Unlike overindulgent parents, mentoring parents do not force their unmet dreams onto their children. They realize that children, who aim for their parents' unmet goals and dreams, lose the opportunity to acquire their own dreams, which is the goal of self-reliance.

Mentoring parents actively pursue their dreams throughout life. Watching parents strive toward goals and dreams is an excellent quality for children to model. Mentoring parents encourage their children to pursue their goals and dreams, and offer support as well as constructive criticism to encourage their children's sense of accomplishment and self-reliance.

Rationalizations and Insights About Talents and Skills:

Some overindulgent parents believe their children have the same needs and dreams they had when they were children. So, they try to make their children happy by giving them what they wanted when they were children. This results in giving children what parents wanted and not what children need. This is like trying to put a three-prong plug into a two-prong outlet. Despite their best efforts, no real connection occurs.

Many overindulgent parents believe their children cannot attain self-reliance. So they stop their children from taking the risks necessary to become self-reliant. One 12-year-old child I counseled had a serious bully problem. Bullies usually isolate vulnerable children before they hurt them. So, managing a bully demands self-reliance because no one is available to help. His overindulgent mother stopped him from learning how to manage bullies.

This 12-year-old boy's mother thought it was unfair that this much larger bully was picking on her son. Instead of mentoring her child, she took the reigns. She marched her son to the bully's home, confronted his parents and threatened legal action if the bullying persisted. The bullying got worse, of course, because the bully used the mother's ranting as leverage for more hazing. Now the bully called her son a wimp, because his mommy had to help him.

This 12-year-old boy did not learn how to handle bullies. When he becomes an adult and his employer is not fair, his mother cannot confront his employer. He will not know what to do, because he was taught to have his mother handle it. He needs advice—and experience— on handling bullies now, so he can become self-reliant as an adult.

A policeman mentored a teenager with a very difficult bully problem, by promoting self-reliance. Everyday after school, five teens would harass and threaten a 15-year-old boy. His concerned parents talked to the police. Of course, there was little they could do because the harassing boys had not committed any illegal action. His parents became very frustrated.

The police know that bullies isolate people, so no one can help. One of the policemen asked the boy this very important question, "In the group of five boys that are bothering you, does the smallest boy have the biggest mouth. Usually if there is a group of kids, the smallest of the group is the instigator. Is that the case?"

The boy said that it was the case. The police continued, "Well if that is the case, here is my best suggestion. Call this boy out and tell him you will fight him one-on-one." The boy did and the instigator backed down with trembling fear. Now that's mentoring. Did you notice that the policeman's idea felt risky. Well, life is not risk-free and to manage life, children need to take risks.

Quality #4: Unconditional Love

Mentoring parents strive to offer children unconditional love, but mentoring parents do not define unconditional love as children getting and doing whatever they want. They also understand that unconditional love means allowing children to experience the consequences of their misbehavior. Mentoring parents realize that consequences help children create self-guidance.

Mentoring parents do not confuse unconditional love with permissiveness and a lack of discipline. They realize their children need to experience the consequences of their misbehavior.

I am sure you recall this hazing incident reported by the national news. Every year, high school girls hazed other girls at a football game with no injuries and no problems. The hazing was usually good fun. In this case, the girls turned vicious. The victims had gashes in their heads requiring stitches. The aggressors felt justified in hurting the girls and continued with extreme aggression.

But did you know that some of their parents went to their State Supreme Court to get their children out of the consequences that the school invoked. Wow!

∽⫘∾

In another example, several high school students attacked other students. In their rush to hurt others they hurt innocent families and children. The entire incident was recorded on videotape. The school suspended the students for their extreme violent behavior. A major political figure arrived on the scene with the goal of getting these violent students out of their suspension.

Let your children experience the full consequences of their misbehavior. If you buffer your children from the consequences of their misbehavior, your children's behavior will get worse.

Teach your children to manage life within the rules of our society. When a child hits another child, an overindulgent parent makes excuses for the child or blames someone else. A mentoring parent considers it a self-centered act and disciplines.

Rationalizations for Buffering Consequences:

Many overindulgent parents rationalize, "My children are so unique and special, they should not follow the same rules as everyone else." This rationalization creates self-centered children. Mentoring parents understand that while they view their children as unique and talented, they require their children to follow the rules of school and home.

Many overindulgent parents believe that experiencing consequences for misbehavior will hurt their children's self-esteem. They fear their children will become unhappy and dissatisfied if they have to face consequences for their actions. So, overindulgent parents take a protective stance and stop appropriate consequences for their children.

Insights for the Mentoring Parent:

Children who never feel the discomfort of consequences for their misbehavior become self-centered. They believe they can do anything and get away with anything. They view their parents as tools, designed to get them out of trouble.

To gain influence with children, predict what will happen to them if they continue to misbehave. Your children may not believe your predictions. When your predictions come true, your children will begin to trust you.

Quality #5: Normal Emotions Are Healthy Emotions

Mentoring parents realize that children need to feel and express normal emotions. Normal emotions are healthy emotions and have messages, which contribute to children's self-guidance and self-reliance.

Normal emotions are emotions that naturally fit a situation. If children experience a joyous event, the natural emotion would be joy. If they experience a loss, the natural emotions would be an array of grief emotions. If they experience a crisis, the natural emotions would be crisis reactions. If they are victimized by violence, the natural emotions would be trauma reactions.

Children do not realize that all normal emotions exist for a reason. When children feel uncomfortable emotions, they need a mentoring parent to attach good thinking to their normal but uncomfortable emotions.

If children do not understand their normal emotions, they have a natural tendency to attach distorted thinking to them. So, when children feel the normal emotions of grief after a family pet or loved one dies, they may think, "What's wrong with me?" A mentoring parent attaches good thinking to children's grief emotions by assuring them that these uncomfortable emotions are normal and expected. When children experience normal emotions that are pleasant or unpleasant, mentoring parents teach children valuable lessons.

Twelve-year-old Jeremy and his uncle had great fun together on his uncle's ranch. Jeremy spent every weekend with his uncle who he dearly loved. When his uncle died in a car accident, Jeremy was devastated.

*His parents hated to see him suffer, and it was tempt-
ing to overindulge Jeremy to console him. However,
they resisted this temptation. Instead, they told him
they understood his anguish, and assured him that
anguish was a natural emotion to feel when losing a
loved one. They encouraged him to remember all the
neat and wonderful gifts his uncle gave him, the time
they spent together, the fun, support, memories, and
affection. They told him that it was perfectly normal
for him to feel anguish because he missed his uncle.
They told Jeremy they felt the same anguish too.*

Instead of trying to distract Jeremy with new toys and
fun activities, his mentoring parents taught Jeremy how to
grieve. Jeremy bonded with his parents, because they
accepted his grief.

Due to his parents' guidance, Jeremy will be able to
handle other difficult life experiences. His parents provided
the mentoring and direction he needed to build the healthy
management of emotions.

Rationalizations for Erasing Normal, but Uncomfortable Emotions:

Overindulgent parents distract their children from natural, but uncomfortable emotions. They believe they can
relieve children's emotional pain with the quick-fix happiness of overindulgence. Some overindulgent parents believe
that if they alter reality, they can stop their children from
feeling painful emotions. So, overindulgent parents tell
children Grandpa is sleeping when Grandpa is dead. They
tell their children the family dog is missing, instead of the
truth that their dog is dead.

Insights for the Mentoring Parent:

Mentoring parents help children face reality together, and teach them the meaning of uncomfortable emotions. Truth, combined with good thinking, helps children understand their natural emotions and helps them learn to manage life.

Children need important instruction about their emotions. Get a children's dictionary and look up the words of various emotions. A children's dictionary has a simple way of describing emotions that children understand. When you see your children feeling embarrassment, grief reactions, or any other uncomfortable emotions, tell your children the name of these emotions and why they exist. Children need to know that their emotions are natural and normal.

Quality #6: "Wants" vs. "Needs"

Mentoring parents know the difference between children's "needs" and children's "wants for luxuries".

Loving parents fulfill their children's needs (safeguarding their children's life, offering love, giving affection), but they feel no need to fulfill their children's "wants for luxuries" (expensive activities, college, investments, toys, cars). As I mentioned earlier, children's "want for luxuries" has nothing to do with parental love or with the quality of family relationships. Mentoring parents express love, without giving expensive luxury items to their children. They show love with hugs and loving touch. They have a natural interest and loving investment of time with their children:

- By helping children learn their talents and skills.
- By gradually offering freedom to children as they become older and more responsible.
- By inviting them to believe in God.
- By giving them good thinking when they have uncomfortable emotions.
- By practicing the qualities of a mentoring parent.
- By always being a genuine and honest parent.
- By helping children correct their flaws.

Our generation of parents is having the greatest difficulty with overindulging children with wants (expensive activities and luxuries), while ignoring children's needs (especially the depth of instruction about life that mentoring parents can offer). To reduce excessive "giving" to your children I have a suggestion that will help you create a better relationship with your children. Give your children gifts on birthdays and holidays only! This is a difficult instruction for overindulgent parents to fulfill, but a worthy one. If you follow this suggestion, it forces you to connect with your children beyond the "marketing" definition of happiness.

Overindulgence spoils children and damages family bonding. When parents overindulge their children, parents tie their worthiness as parents to their purse strings. Overindulged children view their parents as wonderful when they overindulge, and less than wonderful when they refuse to overindulge. In effect children are saying, "You are a worthy parent when you give me things, and unworthy when you do not." Refuse to overindulge your children. Always remember, you do not need to overindulge children to have a loving relationship.

Rationalizations for Giving Too Much:

There is a portion of marketing media that complicates parenting. Marketing media wants to make profit. One way to make profit in marketing is to drive a wedge between parents and their children. This is accomplished by a certain segment of marketing that uses the "Nag Effect." The "Nag Effect" creates idealized parents in television commercials, which are parents that will let their children do anything. When actual parents do not live up to the idealized parents presented on television commercials, children nag at their parents.

Here is an example of the "Nag Effect." Several years ago there was a television commercial about hip-hugger jeans. A girl, looking 13 years of age, was wearing hip-huggers and getting ready for school. Her idealized mom spots the low-cut pants and says, Oh no!" Then the idealized mom pulls her daughters' hip-huggers down and says, "That's better!" When actual parents say, "Wear something more appropriate!" actual parents seem ridiculous to their children, because of the influence of idealized parents in television commercials. So children start nagging at their parents.

Overindulgent parents bend to this pressure created by media marketing. In fact, many parents see these commercials and believe they represent what good parents should do. Overindulgent parents are seeking approval from the children. When they see the happy smiles of their children after receiving another toy or fun activity, they believe they are doing their job as parents. Their children appear happy.

Insights for the Mentoring Parent:

Don't bend to outside forces. Children constantly criticize mentoring parents for not being flexible, like their friends' parents. When you hear that comment from your children, you are doing your job. Realize that not only media create pressure on you to overindulge your children; there is a greater pressure – parent pressure.

When I was a child and I wanted a toy or asked for a freedom too soon, I would often say, "So and so got one" or "My buddy is getting to go." Usually this was not true. Today it is true. Parents are giving their children more stuff and more freedoms, too fast and too soon. This creates parent pressure on mentoring parents. Parents, who let their children do anything, indirectly put pressure on parents who are not overindulging their children.

Stand your ground. I have traveled throughout this country talking to many parents about overindulgence. Adult-children often tell their parents that restricting them and setting limits when they were children were good things!

Quality #7: The Past, Present, and Future

The past does not control mentoring parents because they understand how their past influences the present and the future.

The field of psychology has missed an important opportunity in the last twenty years. When treating adults with childhood issues, many mental health clinicians of the 1980s focused on rehashing their adult-clients' past, such as childhood issues. Often current concerns and planning for the future were ignored.

I believe some past-oriented counselors directed adult-clients into an aimless and self-centered focus on their unmet childhood needs. Much of this prompted adults to view themselves as victims of their childhood, when they were not victims at all.

Instead of an obsession with childhood issues, parents need to review their past (not obsess about it) and consider its impact on their present life and future. In other words, consider this question: "How will reflecting on the past create a better life now and in the future for you and your family?"

Mentoring parents do not obsess about their past nor do they define themselves as victims, because they have a clear direction in their lives. This makes them attractive leaders that children will naturally want to follow. Mentoring parents appreciate the good and bad experiences from their past, learning from it instead of becoming victims.

Sometimes there is true abuse that occurred in parents' childhoods. But even true abuses should not restrict a mentoring parents ability to gain insight and adapt.

Debra was truly abused as a child. Her abusive childhood interfered with her parenting. She was not the parent she wanted to be for her children. Because of her past abuse, she was so overprotective that she stopped her children from experiencing a normal life. She restricted her children from enjoying childhood.

She realized she was overprotective, but she could not control it. Concerned for her ability as a parent, she sought counseling to review her past. One of her goals was to release herself from her over-protectiveness, so she could be a better parent.

As she reviewed her abusive past, she remembered that as a child she grieved the loss of having normal childhood experiences. She remembered losing the freedom to invite friends for overnights and parties, and recalled how the abuse kept her away from many fun activities with her friends.

Her counselor helped Debra realize that her over-protectiveness offered the same severe limitations to her children. Debra became a mentoring parent the day she used this insight to lower her over-protective-ness and allow her children to have their childhood.

⌒⧘⌒

Whenever family problems occurred, Dennis' parents lied to him. They believed they were protecting him. As a child, instead of hearing that a relative died, the relative mysteriously disappeared from Dennis' life without explanation. When there were obvious stresses in his parents' relationship, his parents refused to talk. All of this protectiveness made Dennis isolate from his parents.

When Dennis became a parent, he also withheld information from his children. Of course, when children feel family tensions and have no explanation, they often conjure up feelings of responsibility and guilt. Through counseling, Dennis was able to recall his childhood insecurities and realized he created the same feelings of confusion, guilt, and shame in his children. He rehearsed being more open and honest with his children. His children immediately responded thankfully to his openness. Dennis was becoming a mentoring parent.

In the accounts above, both Debra and Dennis reviewed their past, changed their present life, and looked forward to a brighter future as mentoring parents. Instead of obsessing about past abuses or tensions, they gained insights into their old issues, which helped them create positive changes in their lives and the lives of their children. Both parents could have chosen to wallow in anger over their imperfect childhoods, but that makes lousy parents. Instead, they gained insights from their past, which helped to create good relationships with their children.

Insights for the Mentoring Parent:

Some parents have real abuse issues in their childhood. Others exaggerate their abuse. Whether the abuse was real or exaggerated, what parents do with these issues is important. Instead of breeding angry, use that energy to make positive changes in your life and the lives of children.

Quality #8: Realistic Understanding Of Strengths and Limits – Yours and Your Children

Mentoring parents realize that having strengths and limits is a normal human condition. They have a realistic appraisal of their own personal strengths and limits, and give their children a realistic and hopeful appraisal of their strengths and limits as well.

Mentoring parents are usually humble and modest. They do not brag, but they can correctly describe their accomplishments and failures. When parents know their strengths and limits, they never exaggerate their talents or their children's talents. In fact, they know exaggeration leads to distorted labels, which harms children.

Consider this distorted label: How many parents do you know that believe they have a gifted child? Research says that only 3% of the population is gifted, but I believe every third parent I talk to has a gifted child! Often they have a bright child, not a gifted child. So, the label "gifted" is a distorted label when it is applied to a non-gifted child. Before entering school, many overindulgent parents convince their children they are gifted. This is a set-up for a humiliating experience. These children learn, in a public arena (school), that they are not gifted at all.

Mentoring parents help their children realize their individuality without distorted labels such as "gifted." They spend quality time with their children, helping them understand their strengths and limits. They honestly praise the strengths of their children and realistically encourage them to improve their talents and skills.

> *Joey was never going to be a mathematician, since he could not decipher even the easiest math problems. His mother was a practical mentor who was honest with Joey. She would often tell him stories of great people in history who had limits: Einstein with his learning disability; Churchill with his childhood behavior problems; and Roosevelt with his physical disability. Joey's mother described these people as having great talents, but also great limits. She would often say to him, "Our wonderful talents make us feel good about ourselves, and our limits keep us humble." Being a realist, she reminded Joey of his advanced ability to read. She also gave him a calculator and affectionately said, "You're going to need this." The gift she offered Joey was the realistic opportunity to honor his talents and accept his limits. But perhaps her greatest gift was accepting Joey as he was.*

Rationalizations for Distorting Strengths and Limits:

Mentoring parents, like Joey's mother, are accepting of their children, but they encourage their children to progress and adapt with their limits. Continually assess your children's strengths and limits and offer them positive and productive suggestions.

When overindulgent parents see their children as perfect, they ignore the real limits of their children. They fail to give their children instruction on how to adapt with their limits. Their prevailing thought is, "If my child is perfect, there are no limits to correct." This distorted view stops parents from managing the real limits of their children. It removes the first step of correction—identifying children's limits.

When overindulgent parents pamper their children, their children never hear any real constructive criticisms until they go to school. This, of course, puts their children at a severe academic disadvantage. Since they do not know how to manage constructive criticism, they either ignite in anger or ignore their teachers.

Insights for the Mentoring Parent:

Mentoring parents accept their children as individuals, but they strive to include a realistic look at their strengths and limits. Like Joey's mother, mentoring parents promote their children's natural talents and strive to give them real solutions to compensate for their limits. When mentoring parents teach their children how to manage their limits, they are saying, "I will lovingly teach you to compensate and work toward overcoming your limits. It is a gift for you." When this happens, children learn to accept their limits and they feel accepted by their parents. These children more readily communicate with adults, such as teachers, counselors, principals, police officers, and employers.

Take a moment to recall someone in your life who cared enough to be honest with you, even with sensitive issues. That's a real mentor! Offer loving statements when you mention a child's limitation. Make a list of the strengths and limits within your children. Plan and rehearse how to honestly praise your children's strengths as well as encourage them to adapt with their limitations.

Quality #9: Respect For All

Mentoring parents promote respect for all groups.

Mentoring parents are respectful to all groups of people and encourage their children to do the same. This does not mean that mentoring parents agree with everyone and every lifestyle. They have various opinions based on their values and views about controversial topics. Mentoring parents can passionately discuss, debate, and disagree about hot controversial topics (such as homosexuality, abortion, right to die), but still offer respect and appreciation for those who disagree with them.

Mentoring parents express their opinions, but they refrain from one-upmanship, revenge, or retaliation. They do not become obnoxious with those who disagree with them. They are passionate about their opinions, but they feel no need to force opinions onto others. They are usually very influential with their children because they teach them how to develop their own opinions, rather than force children to agree with them.

> *Tom was politically conservative and his college daughter was ultraliberal. Because they did not agree on any of the hot political issues, they had heated but respectful discussions about abortion, right to die, environmental issues, and more—but never got angry at each other. Tom allowed his daughter the freedom to explore many ideas and opinions. He did not feel*

threatened by her contrary views. When he considered his boyhood, he recalled having many of the same ideas as his daughter. He also recalled how important those ideas were to him. He realized his daughter was entitled to her views, and he respected her views.

⟜⟝

Marilyn loved both of her children equally, but one of her sons was more difficult and required more attention, overseeing and discipline. Because she could express love and affection equally, both of her children felt her love, and recognized one might receive more attention from time-to-time.

Mentoring parents appreciate people's differences in culture and background, as well as within their families. They see all people as equal, and teach their children to accept others. They also love their children equally and teach them to care for others. However, they realize that loving their children equally does not mean they raise their children the same. Children are unique and deserve the right to be raised according to their uniqueness.

Rationalizations for Not Respecting Others:

Let's be honest! Overindulgent parents see their children as superior to others, and competitively compare and contrast their children with others. They focus on proving their children's superiority, which means that they ignore their children's limits and flaws. They also believe there is no need to correct their children, because their children are perfect. Due to their special beliefs about their children, they expect others (such as teachers, counselors, principals) to grant their children special privileges. They promote the idea their children are the exceptions to the rules.

Insights for the Mentoring Parent:

Give your children the freedom to be different, and to express their ideas and opinions. Allowing this free exchange helps children develop their individuality and social skills. As children mature, they will remember your openness to their ideas and advice. It is amazing to see children become adults and accept their parents' ideas about how to live life. But this only happens with a free exchange of ideas.

It is a great idea to expose children to other cultures. This helps children learn there are culture-specific reasons people from different countries act in different ways. This creates children who are tolerant of others and appreciate the diversity other cultures offer.

Quality #10: Values

Mentoring parents have well-defined values and practice their values daily.

Mentoring parents carry their values with them everywhere. Their values are constant and stable. They do not separate their "self" from their behavior, and their behavior always reflects their values. So, parents who practice their values can go anywhere (church, casino, tavern, park, work, and home) and they act with integrity. Couples, who exercise good basic values, trust their partners because their partners have good moral values, ethics, and loyalty to the marital relationship.

Mentoring parents know that having healthy values makes life less complicated for them and their loved ones. For example, if parents are loyal to each other, they offer a firm foundation for each person in their family to flourish.

Children can predict their parents' reactions when complications in life occur, because mentoring parents are stable and consistent. Parents' stability and consistency are especially important since children learn most of their values by watching their parents. When parents are inconsistent with their values, children become confused. When parents have stable values, children feel more secure. For example, if both parents are honest, children feel stable; if one parent is dishonest children become confused and insecure.

Although our culture seems to be losing this idea, mentoring parents realize their behavior is a reflection of their values. Mentoring parents value taking responsibility for their actions and make no excuses. They enforce that their children also take responsibility for their actions, which includes the consequences for misbehavior.

Mentoring parents have a firm commitment to basic values (safety, honesty, authenticity), which are essential for family members. They also have a deep commitment toward values that create individual differences and define each family member's personality. Mentoring parents understand that values are foundational for healthy families, that values have a purpose, and allow children to feel stable and secure in their relationship with their parents.

Rationalizations for a Lack of Basic Values:

"You cannot tell me my values," is a comment that many adults and children make today. They believe it is their individual right to pick their values, which it is. However, without the basic values of safety, trust, fidelity, affiliation, acceptance, honesty, and fairness, it is impossible to have good relationships with others. Families without core values have no foundation. Their children become so concerned about the lack of values that they cannot adequately function.

Overindulgent parents believe their children have values, whether they do or not. For example, they are convinced their children would not hurt anyone, in spite of obvious evidence that they did hurt someone. Overindulgent parents overlook their children's misbehavior and lack of values, thinking, "My child is a good child and would never do bad behavior."

Insights for the Mentoring Parent:

Feel free to express your values with your children. Be careful to not stomp on their ideas as they dialog with you. Remember that your children's ideas are changing. Their ideas are in motion and not solidified. Give your children the safety and freedom to share their ideas with you.

Summary

You now have the overindulgent parenting principles and the qualities of the mentoring parent. In the next chapter, let's use these overindulgent parenting beliefs to analyze your responses to your children's misbehavior. Then, we will use the qualities of the mentoring parent to help you effectively change your parenting to become a mentoring parent.

~ CHAPTER 4 ~

The Mystery of Children's Misbehavior—Solved

All children misbehave. Take a moment and remember your greatest blunders when you were a child. Misbehaving is a natural part of childhood. Your reactions to your children's misbehavior are critical.

One significant problem is that overindulgent parents minimize their children's misbehavior. This leads overindulgent parents to under-react to their children's misbehavior, which increases their children's misbehavior. One reason overindulgent parents under-react is a lack of awareness of the purposes of common misbehaviors.

In this chapter, you will learn these purposes. This chapter teaches you how to replace overindulgent parenting with the qualities of the mentoring parent. As we discuss each common behavior problem, we also will discuss which of the overindulgent parenting beliefs encourage specific misbehaviors. Then, using the qualities of the mentoring parent, I will give you suggestions to correct your children's misbehaviors

Back-Talk

The Purpose of Back-Talk:

Children who back-talk want power. Back-talk is a verbal punch. So, children use back-talk to hurt or control others. Since their back-talk is nasty, they are also seeking revenge. Overindulgent parents give-in to back-talking children, which gives children too much power. When children realize the power of back-talk, they grab for more power by using more back-talk.

Some children use back-talk to push their parents' buttons, which ignites their parents into an explosive tirade. After the tirade, overindulgent parents feel guilty. The combination, of tirade and guilt, leads overindulgent parents to excessively give-in to their children. When overindulgent parents give-in, they feel relieved from their guilt for their tirade. This combination (children back-talking and parents raging and giving-in) becomes ingrained and creates difficult families.

All children will occasionally back-talk, but back-talking becomes severe when overindulgent parents do not correct it. Consider these overindulgent parenting beliefs, which increase children's back-talk.

Overindulgent Parenting Beliefs That Encourage Back-Talking:

Whatever You Want! Overindulgent parents believe that unconditional love means children should receive and do whatever they want.

Many overindulgent parents are loving parents who want their children to have all possible advantages. They work to make advantages available to their children. Unfortunately, they believe letting their children back-talk is one of the advantages their children should have. They believe that if their children want to back-talk, it is fine, as overindulgent parents promote the belief, "Do whatever you want!"

This unrestrained back-talk travels into classrooms. Back-talking children who back-talk parents also back-talk teachers, school principals, and other adults in positions of authority. When children extend their back-talking into the classroom, they complicate their school life. Back-talking prevents children from building mutual relationships with classmates and teachers.

Shield from Consequences: Overindulgent parents shield their children from the consequences of their children's actions, as well as the complications of life.

Overindulgent parents pamper their back-talking children by buffering them from the consequences of their back-talk. Their overindulged children expect this same pampering from others. In other words, since their parents did not give them consequences for back-talking, these children do not expect consequences from other adults.

Juanita back-talked all authority figures and she enjoyed it. Back-talking made her feel powerful and in control of every interaction. She back-talked her parents, teachers, principal, and any other authority figure she believed needed to suffer her wrath. However, when she back-talked her high school principal, her principal disciplined her with a detention. When she back-talked her high school principal again, the principal gave her Saturday School (a deeper form of detention from 7:00am to 11:00 a.m. Saturday morn-

*ing). When she back-talked her principal a third time,
her principal suspended her from school for three days.*

*Juanita believed that when she back-talked she
was in-charge. She refused to accept that back-talking
was helping her lose control of her life. Her back-
talking got her the attention of her school principal,
who dictated real consequences (detentions, Saturday
school, and suspension). Juanita's mother needed to
teach Juanita that back-talking created problems.
Instead, her overindulgent mother attempted to stop
the principal's discipline. She worked hard to shield
her daughter from the consequences that Juanita
earned because of her obstinacy.*

*I Will Correct My Parents' Mistakes: Overindul-
gent parents believe that their parents raised
them improperly, so they long to correct their own
parents' mistakes by becoming perfect parents.*

When some overindulgent parents were children, their
parents restricted their freedom to speak by strictly enforc-
ing the adage "children are to be seen and not heard." Some
parents, who grew up in this strict environment, try to correct their parents' mistake by going to the other extreme.
They give their children complete freedom to speak. Unfortunately, these parents become too permissive and allow
their children to back-talk by advancing the belief, "I will
correct my parents' mistakes by giving my child complete
freedom!" In reality, they are creating a whole new set of
mistakes.

A Mentoring Parent's Management of Children's Back-Talk:

Once you discover which of the overindulgent parenting beliefs you are using, replace your overindulgent beliefs by using the qualities of the mentoring parent. Consider the following suggestions to help mentor your children when they back talk. Notice that the suggestions that reflect the qualities of the mentoring parent are in bold highlight:

Mentoring parents realize they can **unconditionally love** their children, while **teaching limits** to their children. Help your children realize there is a point where self-expression becomes harmful to others, and back-talk crosses that line. In fact, when children back-talk they create conditional love. Many children use back-talk to pressure parents to give them what they want. Here is their conditional message, "When you give me what I want, you will be a good parent and I will stop back-talking—for a while."

Stop your children from back-talking. Ignoring your children's back-talk is one technique, but it varies in its effectiveness. In fact, it is generally ineffective, because other children may encourage your back-taking child.

Another technique involves making children's back-talk ineffective. When children back-talk, they usually want something. What they want usually falls into three categories: toys, permissions, and activities. Mentoring parents **never give back-talking children what they want.**

If your children's back-talking persists, confront your back-talking children by explaining the tactics they are using. Say to your children, "You are back-talking to get this toy, and you will never get it by back-talking." Then stick to this statement.

You can teach your children how to get what they want. As a rule of thumb, the most suitable means for children getting what they want is **work, hard work.**

I would like everyone to get what they want in life, especially children. To get what they want, your children should work. Work is a healthy means for children getting what they want and a great replacement for destructive back-talk and overindulgence.

If you tried to correct your children's back-talk and they continue, allow your children to suffer the **full consequences** of their back-talk. If your child back-talks the football coach and the coach kicks your child off the team, do not rescue your child. Instead, **predict** for your child that these consequences will occur well before they actually happen. When your predictions come true, your child will see you as a mentor and a powerful force in changing their behavior and attitude. In order for your predictions to come true, you need to allow your children to suffer the consequences of their back-talking.

Mentoring parents do considerable predicting for their children. Prediction also keeps children from inflating their self-esteem, believing they know more than their parents. Parents' predictions keep children humble, which is a good quality that needs more practice.

The past does not control mentoring parents. Mentoring parents will not let their own parent's strict parenting style hurt the parenting of their own children by being too permissive. If you have old issues that affect your current life as a parent, fix those old issues—even if it requires counseling. Mentoring parents will not allow old wounds to hurt the parenting of their children. They will get counseling if necessary, to **change old wounds into useful parenting tools.**

Finally, mentoring parents have **respect for all people.** They realize that back-talk is disrespectful, and advise their children to make amends to anyone they have disrespected.

Sulking, Nagging and Whining

The Purpose of Sulking, Nagging, and Whining:

Most overindulgent parents have caring hearts and will do anything to stop their children's sulking—and their children know it. When a child's lip sticks out in a pouting fashion, he or she is sulking. Sulking is a manipulative tool children use to gain attention, special activities, and toys.

Sulking is a child's body language screaming, "Make me happy again, by giving me what I want!" Children use nagging and whining to put pressure on parents to give-in to their demands. The strategy of nagging and whining is that it grates on parents' nerves or pushes "guilt buttons" pressuring parents to give-in. Children's nagging and whining increases because they know these behaviors pay off. But they never know when the payoff will happen because the payoffs are like winning a jackpot or a lottery. Not knowing when a payoff might happen makes this game more enticing.

Parents who give-in to their children's sulking, nagging, and whining employ one or a combination of the following overindulgent parenting beliefs:

Constant Happiness: Overindulgent parents believe that they can create good self-esteem in their children if their children are constantly happy.

Many overindulged children give their parents this message: "Make me happy by giving me the best, so I can be the best." Many parents bite into this fantasy.

The biggest and best sulker, I ever met in my career, was a 17-year-old hockey player. This boy loved hockey, but his skills were not strong. He would never become a professional hockey player. He promoted the belief that to become a better hockey player, he needed the "best" equipment. Unfortunately, his parents bought into this belief, thinking that the best equipment would make him happy and increase his self-esteem.

Even though he was 17 years old, he never had a job. Instead of working to get the best hockey equipment, the 6' 7" 250-pound teenager would stick out his big lip and sulk and whine to his parents. They saturated him with the best hockey equipment money could buy.

I suggested that their son needed to get a part-time job to help pay for his hockey equipment. When he heard my suggestion, the manlike boy gawked at his parents with his stuck out lip, whining, "He wants me to work at some place like a WalMart!" The couple looked at their son with sympathetic eyes and his mother came to tears. Then they looked at me as if they were looking at an ogre!

Overindulgent parents believe that normal expectations (such as work) are abnormal for their "special" children. Instead of working, their children sulk, nag, and whine. Unfortunately, there is an undercurrent of permissiveness in our culture that reinforces whining and self-indulgence. Our "pop culture" heavily rewards its heroes for their excessive whining and self-indulgence. Consider the examples of sports and entertainment personalities who do whatever they want, no matter who it hurts, because they think they are "special." Children see celebrities' whininess and self-indulgence continually rewarded with money, movie contracts, and endorsements. It seems misguided celebrities can get away with anything and continue their professional lives without real consequences.

The idiocy of our "pop culture" is tough competition for parents who try to convince their children that misbehavior does not pay. What children do not realize is the rarity of special privileges for the arrogant and uncouth celebrities of this world. Children, especially young and impressionable children, need parents to teach them that important fact.

Wishy-Washy Decisions: Overindulgent parents have difficulty with firm decisions and usually make wishy-washy decisions when they do.

Many parents believe that when children sulk and whine, they should negotiate with their children to help feel they are part of the decision-making process. There is a fundamental problem that makes negotiating with nagging and whining children nearly impossible. When parents negotiate, their goal is to achieve fairness for both parties.

Nagging and whining children are immature and they only want to win! Negotiation is an excellent technique with most teenagers, when they are mature enough to be fair with negotiations, but it does not work with nagging, whining, and immature children who want to win. When parents give-in to nagging and whining children, parents become wishy-washy! Don't give-in!

Too Trusting: Overindulgent parents are too trusting.

When parents are too trusting, they become gullible. When children sulk, their pain and sadness are not real. Overindulgent parents gullibly react to their children's best portrayal of pain and sadness, as if these portrayals are real emotions. When parents gullibly believe their children's fake emotions are real, power transfers from parents to children. The emotional pull of being too trusting is that sulking children make their parents feel guilty so parents will give-in.

One seven-year-old boy, whose mother I eventually trained as a mentoring parent, was an expert at creating so much guilt within his mother that he influenced her decisions. When in a department store with his mother, he begged for a new toy. Initially, his mother refused to buy it. When she finally gave-in the boy said, "I don't want it." Despite her pleas for him to reconsider, he refused. She felt even more guilt. This boy was training his mother to say "Yes" the first time he asked.

A Mentoring Parent's Management of Children's Sulking, Nagging, and Whining

Once you discover which of the overindulgent parenting beliefs you are using when your children sulk and whine, you can replace those distorted beliefs by reviewing the qualities of the mentoring parent. Consider the following ideas and suggestions to mentor your sulking, nagging, and whiny children. As before, the following suggestions that reflect the qualities of the mentoring parent are in bold highlight:

Mentoring parents are immune to their children's sulking, nagging, and whining. They know that children's **sulking, nagging, and whining are not real emotions,** but manipulative games.

Ignore your children's attempts to manipulate with sulking, nagging, and whining. If you give-in —even once—to your children's fake emotions, their sulking, nagging, and whining will dramatically increase. To help children reduce sulking, nagging, and whining, do not buy them anything. If your children ask for special toys or activities when they are upset, your children are manipulating you. **Love and affection soothe real emotional pain,** but buying is not a requirement. Put your pocket book away!

Mentoring parents have a **heartfelt commitment to truth and reality.** When children sulk, nag, and whine, tell your children that they are faking emotions to get what they want. Tell your children they will never get what they want when they sulk, nag, and whine. Could you imagine sulking, nagging and whining to your boss to get a raise? Of course not! What do you do when you want something? You work for it. Redirect your children to work for what they want by telling them, "I will show you how you can earn what you want, but I am not giving it to you." This redirection toward work teaches children that they can gain empowerment by working. When in doubt, make them work!

Giving-in to children teaches them to be over-dependent. Mentoring parents want their children to receive all the wonderful experiences in life, but they want their children to earn what they get.

When parents teach their children to work, they are also teaching their children to save money, learn to be responsible, plan their finances, preserve their belongings, fulfill commitments, and many more important skills. Overindulged children only learn to be dependent and to enjoy life's indulgences.

Crying

Purpose of Crying:

There are many sincere, as well as insincere, reasons for crying. Sincere crying can be a release of hurt, a release of frustration, an expression of helplessness, as well as an expression of happiness. For many children, the purpose of their crying is innocent, but how parents react to their children's tears could determine if their crying remains innocent.

There are two types of crying: sincere and insincere. Often, young children cry sincere tears when they are physically or emotionally hurt. Crying becomes insincere when children have an agenda other than the release of hurt. For example, when one of my children was small, his brother had a blanket that he wanted, so he cried at the top of his lungs. When his brother gave him the blanket, his crying stopped as quickly as turning off a faucet. Real emotional pain does not clear up that quickly. Children use insincere crying to gain attention and manipulate others.

Overindulgent parents react to their children's insincere crying as if it were sincere crying. When this occurs, children learn that their insincere crying gets them what they want. So, they continue to pretend to be upset.

Many overindulgent parents, who are susceptible to children's insincere crying, often have one or more of the following overindulgent parenting beliefs:

Overindulgent Parenting Principles That Encourage Insincere Crying:

Constant Happiness combined with Whatever You Want: Overindulgent parents believe that they create good self-esteem in their children if their children are constantly happy, They also believe that unconditional love means children should receive whatever they want and do whatever they want.

To squelch children's unhappy emotions, overindulgent parents give their children quick-fix "marketing" happiness. In fact, quick-fix "marketing" happiness for children is much of today's economy. For example, McDonald's sells Happy Meals. Christmas is one long commercial designed to pressure parents to get that one special toy they believe will create perfect happiness for their children. Most parents believe that to make their children happy, they must get their children to Disney World at least once. When they finally get to Disney World, their over-stimulated children become ornery and cranky. This frustrates overindulgent parents who are trying to win their children's happiness.

With such pressure for happiness, crying is the enemy of the overindulgent parent because it says, "Your children are not happy, so they will not have good self-esteem!"

These parents stop their children's crying by becoming even more overindulgent. They give their children whatever they want and let them do whatever they desire.

Shield from Consequences: Overindulgent parents shield their children from the consequences of their actions, as well as the complications of life.

Overindulgent parents pamper their children by shielding them from the consequences of their misbehavior. Overindulged children use insincere crying to motivate parents to stop the consequences children earned.

When overindulgent parents excessively pamper their children, they raise children who acquire no skills. Instead of learning to become self-reliant (which includes managing the consequences of your actions), pampered children learn to use insincere crying. Insincere crying motivates parents to continue pampering their children by buffering them from the consequences of their misbehavior.

A Mentoring Parent's Management of Children's Crying:

Once you discover which of the overindulgent beliefs you are have, consider the qualities of the mentoring parent. So, think about the following ideas and suggestions to mentor your children when they insincerely cry. As always, the suggestions reflecting the qualities of the mentoring parent are in bold highlight:

Mentoring parents, who realize their children are sincerely crying, create an **emotional bond.** They never offer toys and expensive activities to crying children, because they realize these items do not sooth emotions.

Also, mentoring parents debunk the cultural idea that parents should keep their children happy by buffering children from the complications of life. Mentoring parents realize there will always be complications in life that are emotionally sensitive. Mentoring parents **experience and express their natural and normal emotions.** If you understand your own emotions, it is easier to mentor to your children when they have emotional times. Also, if you are in tune with your emotions, you can more easily recognize your children's sincere and insincere crying.

The solution for children's insincere crying is not showering children with toys and expensive activities. Instead, it is helpful to caringly confront and truthfully tell your children that they are playing a manipulative game.

Mentoring parents know that when their children engage in insincere crying, they either want their parents to overindulge them or want to get out of consequences for misbehavior. Mentoring parents never grant children what they want when children perform insincere crying. Redirect your children toward **work and self-reliance,** and teach them to **face the consequences of their actions.**

Mentoring parents realize that childhood cannot be emotionally painless, because life is not emotionally painless. They know that children need to learn how to manage unhappy events in life and the associated uncomfortable emotions. The best that parents can do is to allow children to express emotions with loved ones. Mentoring parents can offer children a **safe atmosphere to express their emotions.**

When overindulgent parents rush to buy their children out of uncomfortable emotions, they are teaching their children that it is not normal to feel natural emotions. Hugs may be less expensive, but they are more powerful. When children hurt, they need **love, affection, and guidance**—not stuff. When children suggest that a new toy or privilege would help heal their pain, it is tempting to try to buy children out of their uncomfortable emotions. Don't do it!

Natural emotions (including uncomfortable emotions) have a purpose, which gives children important information. For example, if your child hurts another child, your child may feel the natural emotion of guilt. This is a good thing! You can **attach good thinking** to your child's emotion of guilt by suggesting that the your child make amends. This relieves your child's guilt and teaches your child to manage emotions and mend relationships.

Remember back! If you had mentoring parents, there were times when they intentionally made you feel bad. If you misbehaved your mentoring parent would say, "This is one of those times you should feel bad. And here is exactly what you need to do to make amends." When you made amends, you felt better. This is the natural emotion of guilt, used to motivate children to behave. This also creates self-guidance. In other words, children learn the thought, "If I do not want to feel guilt, I better make amends." This parental advice becomes the child's thought, which creates self-guidance.

Overindulged children learn to not feel their natural emotions, because they are so distracted with expensive toys and fun activities. Unfortunately, overindulgent parents do not mentor their children, and without mentoring, children do not learn to attach good thinking to their natural emotions and lose good self-guidance. This complicates children's relationships with loved ones and friends, because self-guidance leads children to make amends when they misbehave, and making amends enhances mutual relationships.

Mentoring parents help their children by attaching good thinking to their natural emotions.

Consider the following examples:

- When children feel anguish because a loved one died, mentoring parents explain that anguish is a normal emotion that teaches children how much they loved their lost loved one.
- When children feel embarrassed by their misbehavior, mentoring parents teach children that embarrassment is a signal that they need to change their misbehavior.

Mentoring parents do not mask these uncomfortable emotions with false happiness. Instead, they explain the purposes of each emotion and teach their children to manage their emotions.

Teasing and Bullying

Purposes of Teasing and Bullying:

Like all people, children want status. There is good status and bad status. Good status happens when a child works hard and achieves the honor roll. Unfortunately, some children try to achieve status by using teasing and bullying, which is bad status. For example, when children gain status by teasing and bullying, children push for status at the expense of others. Sadly, this status is shallow and hollow, because no one wants to bond with teasers and bullies.

Overindulgent parents view their children's teasing and bullying in a positive light. They mislabel their children's teasing and bullying as an expression of affection, strength, a positive personality characteristic, or assertiveness. Because overindulgent parents mislabel children's teasing and bullying, teasing and bullying continue. They become lenient with children's teasing and bullying with one or a combination of the following overindulgent parenting beliefs.

Overindulgent Parenting Beliefs That Encourage Teasing And Bullying:

Sting-Free Discipline: Overindulgent parents either offer no discipline or take the sting out of their discipline.

Since overindulgent parents minimize their children's teasing and bullying as a positive characteristic, they see no reason to discipline their children.

One parent I counseled became frustrated with the father of a bullying child. He made many attempts to explain to the bully's father that his son's bullying was too extreme. The father minimized his son's bullying behavior with the phrase, "Boys will be boys," belittling the harshness of the bullying as typical boy behavior.

With his "Boys will be boys" philosophy, his son's bullying continued. This allows parents who are raising bullies to say, "If I see no problem with my child, there is no problem that needs correction." These children will continue to bully without the guiding influence of a mentoring parent.

I Will Correct My Parents' Mistakes: Overindulgent parents believe that their parents raised them improperly and long to correct their own parents' mistakes by becoming perfect parents.

Many parents, raised by strict parents, want to give their children excessive freedom. They try to correct their parents' mistakes by giving their own children too much freedom. Unfortunately, they give their children permission to express themselves completely, which includes hurtful teasing and bullying of others.

A Mentoring Parent's Management of Children's Teasing and Bullying

Once you discover which of the overindulgent parenting beliefs you are using, review the qualities of the mentoring parent. Consider the following ideas and suggestions to help mentor your children when they tease and bully.

Mentoring parents can sort the weeds from the veggies, to use a gardening expression. Mentoring parents **truthfully** define children's good behavior and misbehavior. When mentoring parents learn that their children are teasing and bullying, they do not minimize the nasty impact. Instead, they evaluate this information, the source of the information, and their children, before deciding if there are real concerns with excessive teasing and bullying.

Mentoring parents know their children, because they **spend considerable time** with them. They know if their children have any history of excessive teasing and bullying. Unlike overindulgent parents, mentoring parents do not use blinders. They allow themselves to see their children's flaws, and they deal with **truth and reality.** Mentoring parents do not try to raise perfect children, because they know it is impossible. Mentoring parents know what to do when their children are not so perfect.

Once you determine that your children are teasing and bullying, become **proactive. Create consequences** for your children when they tease and bully. Also allow your children to **experience the full consequences** that come with being a bully. This usually includes school discipline, as school authorities often discipline bullies.

Offer a comprehensive response to your children's teasing and bullying by contacting many resources. For example, one mother organized a meeting with her child's teacher, principal, and school counselor to coordinate a plan of action. This resulted in all parties consistently disciplining her child when he bullied other children. That's proactive parenting! That's mentoring at its best!

Tantrums

The Purpose of Tantrums:

A tantrum is a child's "fit" that simply states "I want my way and I want it now!" Tantrums are universal in all cultures and designed to command an audience.

When my own children were younger, I recall one of my children lying on the floor in the living room, wailing his arms and legs on the carpet. My wife and I removed his audience by going into the den. The tantrum suddenly stopped and we heard little footsteps trotting down the hall. He entered the room with dry eyes, laid on the floor and continued with his tantrum. My wife and I calmly talked, ignoring him as his tantrum continued. Since his tantrum was not working, he finally quit.

❦

At one of my parenting seminars, I talked with a mother who told me the traditional story (with a new twist) of her 5-year-old son, who wanted a treat at the grocery store. He spread belly down in the middle of an aisle and started kicking and screaming. She lay down next to him and did the same. He was so embarrassed that he hid so people would not see him with her. That is a daring parent! He did not expect her reaction and he quit performing tantrums in stores.

Our culture has become incredibly materialistic. When a child performs a tantrum in a store, many parents give their children what they want, hoping to stop the tantrums. Buying might stop that one tantrum, but it increases tantrums in the future.

To understand the mindset of overindulgent parents who pay off their tantrum-ridden children, consider the following overindulgent parenting principles.

Overindulgent Parenting Beliefs That Encourage Tantrums:

Whatever You Want! Overindulgent parents believe that unconditional love means children should receive whatever they want and do whatever they want.

When children do not get what they want, they become frustrated. Overindulgent parents try to eliminate their children's frustration with excessive overindulgence, but the road to genuine happiness demands that children learn skills. When parents give children everything they want, children have no need or drive to learn. They only refine one skill: the art of becoming over-dependent on their parents. They refine their over-dependency with the destructive tools of guilt trips, manipulation, excuses, tantrums, anger, intimidation, and a host of other misbehavior. Overindulgent children use tantrums to pressure parents into more and more overindulgence!

Ignore tantrums! You can lead your children to the foundational tools they need when they ask for money, luxuries, and expensive activities. Consider the following examples:

Example 1:
Child: "I want some money."
Parent: "What job are you going to do for it?"

Example 2:
Teenager: "Can I borrow the car?"
Parent: "You can borrow it, if you wash and wax it first."

Example 3:
  Child: "Can my friend stay overnight?"
  Parent: "Only if you spotlessly clean your room."

Example 4:
  Child: "I'm hungry!"
  Parent: "Let's make supper together and then
    do the dishes together."

Review your children's favorite demands, which in the past you quickly fulfilled. In advance, decide which jobs you will require when your children make their demands. Parents often ask me, "Do we have to make them earn everything?" The answer is no, but most children earn nothing. They need to learn to earn most of what they want.

Instead of overindulging children when they have tantrums, create the expectation that your children need to earn a major portion of what they get. This expectation of work is important, because this is how the real world works.

Making children work is difficult for overindulgent parents. Overindulgent parents believe they show love to their children when they overindulge them. Children's tantrums say to parents, "Give me what I want," which is a perfect fit for parents who have difficulty saying, "No." So, parents offer leniency and overindulgence when their children have tantrums, believing they are offering unconditional love.

When overindulgent parents say "No," they feel that they are withholding love. They often feel so badly that they explain to their children their reasons for saying "No." There are times when children need an explanation, and there are times when you should offer no explain to children. When children throw tantrums to get what they want, answer "No" without explanation. Then redirect your children toward work.

Some overindulgent parents do a good job saying "No" to children but then their "No" reduces its sting and becomes a "Maybe." Their "Maybe" eventually becomes a

"Yes." Overindulged children are very persistent, constantly pushing for that "Yes!"

Persistence is a commendable quality when coupled with good and decent motives, but is harmful when attached to manipulation. When children persistently manipulate with tantrums, they will run you ragged and drain your finances.

Mentoring Parents' Management of Children's Tantrums

Once you discover which of the overindulgent parenting beliefs you use, replace them by reviewing the qualities of the mentoring parent. Consider the following ideas and suggestions to mentor children when they throw tantrums.

Mentoring parents offer no audience to children when they perform tantrums. It is best that you offer **no response or an unexpected response** to your children's tantrums. This will stop children from manipulating with tantrums.

Children use tantrums to push parents' buttons (guilt buttons, sympathy buttons, whiny buttons), so they can get a new toy or expensive activity. **Mentoring parents know their own buttons** and can feel when their children have pushed them. When they feel their buttons pushed, mentoring parents create a psychological wall by **slowly contemplating how to respond.** This contemplation stops mentoring parents from acting impulsively, and allows them to either ignore their children's button pushing or create unexpected reactions.

Frustration is a feeling that occurs when children cannot get what they want. Frustration is a good tool! Frustration is an emotion that parents can use to motivate children. Mentoring parents realize that when children become frustrated, children have two choices to relieve their frustration. They can either have a tantrum or **work.**

Tantrums are signals that it is time to **teach your children how to get what they want.** So, children need to **work** instead of performing tantrums. Teach children to ask for odd jobs, so they can earn what they want.

For example, I suggested to one parent that she assign her son five extra jobs throughout the week, which allowed him to have his friend stay for one overnight. I advised another parent that his daughter should accumulate points whenever she baby-sits her sister. Her points allowed her to have more telephone time to call friends during the weekend.

Remember, it is important to insure that children complete all jobs before they get what they want. Offer no advanced credit! Parents should never give their children privileges first with the promise of work later. When children wait, they learn to delay gratification until they earn it. This is the way it is for adults. You work first then you buy later. If not, you accumulate debt.

Children do not realize there are other choices to get what they want. You can teach children to **earn what they want by working.** This helps children create the characteristics of empowerment, self-reliance, and good character.

Blaming and Creating Scapegoats

Purposes of Blaming and Scapegoating:

Occasional blaming of others is typical of all children. When children blame others, they are usually avoiding responsibility for a problem, or they want to avoid a discipline. A solution is to separate children who are blaming one another and place them in a time-out until one confesses.

> When my children were younger they had "blaming- itis." A vase in the living room was broken and I asked, "Who broke the vase?" Both boys pointed firm fingers at each other, singing in harmony, "He did it!" Both were convincing, and it was hard to decide which boy was lying and which was truthful. I told one boy to sit in the den and the other to sit in our bedroom, so they could not talk to each other. I told them, "When the one who is lying tells me the truth, you can both come out of these rooms. Otherwise, you can both stay there all day."
>
> No one spoke for the first hour, or the second hour. During the third hour, one son stuck his head outside the bedroom door and asked, "What's going to happen to the person who did it?" I offered no answer. He asked the same question several times. Again I offered no answer. Then we heard a meek voice say, "I did it." I disciplined the guilty child with additional time-out. He also had to compensate his innocent brother by making his bed for a week.

Occasional blaming is not unusual with children. In its most severe form, scapegoating can become a major family problem. Whoever becomes the scapegoat is given unjust blame for everything that goes wrong in his or her family.

There are real advantages to scapegoating. If there is a family of six and one person is the scapegoat, the other five are off the hook. If one person is the scapegoat, everyone else in the family does not accept responsibility for any family problems. They just blame the scapegoat.

To understand the mindset of parents who scapegoat, let us review the overindulgent parents' beliefs that encourage scapegoating.

Overindulgent Parenting Beliefs That Encourage Scapegoating:

Sting-Free Discipline: Overindulgent parents either offer no discipline or take the sting out of their discipline.

Overindulgent parents scapegoat others instead of holding their children responsible for misbehavior. Without discipline, parents do not give their children caring insight that accompanies good discipline. So, their children continue to scapegoat others.

Children who scapegoat are saying, "If I blame you, I do not have to admit to my own flaws." This distorted conclusion allows children to believe that only other people have flaws. Without parental guidance, they never correct this distorted thought or their behavior.

I Will Correct My Parents' Mistakes: Overindulgent parents believe their parents raised them improperly and long to correct their own parents' mistakes by becoming perfect parents.

Parents who had unhappy childhoods frequently blame their own parents. Parents may or may not have justified reasons for being angry with their own parents. If there is real reason for their anger, parents have no justified reason to wallow in their anger. Parents may have had bad experiences in childhood, but they should not allow those experiences to hurt their own children. When parents continue to blame their own parents (justified or not), children will model their parents' excessive blaming behavior.

Mentoring parents do not ignore their justified anger toward their parents. Instead they work through their anger in counseling, with the goal of improving their current life and future.

Who Am I And Why Am I Here? Overindulgent parents have inadequately developed identities, which hinder their ability to help their children develop their identities. They do not know who they are or why they are here.

Some parents were scapegoats in their families when they were children. Since they were scapegoats, they never had an opportunity to create a real identity. As parents, they continue with their role as a scapegoat, taking the blame for their children's misbehavior. Coupled with being the scapegoat, they often have the distorted belief that if they take the blame, their children will feel better about themselves. Unfortunately, when their children scapegoat others, they do not feel better about themselves. Instead, they compete for a false "king-of-the-hill" status. Many overindulgent children with poor self-esteem constantly fear losing their status. So, they continually scapegoat others to maintain their status.

In her blended family, Beth worried about her "king-of-the-hill" status with her stepbrother and stepsister. To ensure her status, she sabotaged her step-siblings' efforts to please their parents. When they cleaned their bedrooms, she would sneak in and mess up their rooms. Her parents praised Beth for keeping her room clean and disciplined her siblings for having a messy room.

Beth convinced her stepbrother that his sister was messing up his bedroom, which created conflict between them. Because she did not appear to be part of the conflict, she won even higher status with her parents. They believed she was behaving well, especially in comparison to her two step-siblings.

Her need for false status was so strong that she was becoming a mild form of a "Bad Seed." She learned to play manipulative games by pitting people against each other. She played many manipulative games to gain a false sense of status within her family.

A Mentoring Parent's Management of Children Blaming and Creating Scapegoats:

Once you discover which of the overindulgent parenting beliefs you are using, replace them by reviewing the qualities of the mentoring parent. Consider the following ideas and suggestions to help you mentor your children when children blame and scapegoat:

There is a healthy purpose within honest blaming. **Truthful** blame serves this important purpose: if a child misbehaves and accepts blame, the child is taking the first step toward being responsible and making amends. When dishonest blaming occurs, children are setting up scapegoats. Mentoring parents make every attempt to discover the **truth** and discipline children who inappropriately blame others.

The solution for children, who try to create a false status by blaming others, is genuine self-esteem founded on solid skills. When parents **invest in children** by teaching them how to live life to its fullest, there is little need for false status.

Also, mentoring parents do not waste their life losing control of their anger and scapegoating their own parents. When children model angry parents, it is easy for them to scapegoat their parents. If mentoring parents are angry toward their own parents, they are secure enough to enter counseling to resolve their anger.

Lying

The Purposes of Lying:

There are several types of lying, each having a definite purpose:

Exaggeration: Children, who lack confidence, often exaggerate to inflate their self-esteem. Children who exaggerate with wild stories feel like a "gray child," which is a child who does not excel at anything and, therefore, receives little attention. Gray children try to gain attention by telling colorful exaggerations. So, when they exaggerate stories, loved ones offer the enthusiastic attention these children crave.

Distorting the Truth: Distorting the truth is a much more serious lie, because it requires more deception. Children, who distort the truth, often have hidden motives; such as setting up another child to take the blame for their misbehavior; denying the truth to get out of trouble; or avoiding an undesirable activity (homework, chores).

Distorting the truth forces children to continue to lie to keep the original lie believable. With this more advanced lying, children actively rehearse lying and become accomplished liars.

Lying by Omission: When children lie by omission, children withhold important information from their parents, teachers or other authority figures. Lying of this nature is serious, especially if the truth is obvious.

For example:

I counseled a frustrated mother whose 16-year-old son routinely lied by omission. She was waiting for an important phone call, but she needed to run an errand. She instructed her son to take a message and to tell the caller she would call him right back. The caller was her new boyfriend that her son did not like. Her son was angry about his parents' divorce and wanted to punish his mother. So when the boyfriend called, he said his mother would not be home until the next day.

When his mother came home, he intentionally did not mention the phone call to his mother. When later confronted with his omission, he lied again by denying it. He said her boyfriend was trying to create trouble. "Mom, who do you believe, him or me?" His original lie requires continued lying, and continued lying requires a greater commitment to becoming an accomplished liar.

All children occasionally lie, but when children commit to lying, parental intervention is important. Parents can increase their children's lying behavior if they use any of the following overindulgent parenting beliefs.

Overindulgent Parenting Beliefs That
Encourage Lying:

Shield from Consequences: Overindulgent parents shield their children from the consequences of their children's actions as well as the complications of life.

Imagine the complications that occur when parents know their child is lying and protect their child by accepting the child's lie. Consider the following example of a routine middle school science project. The innocuous science project is a good barometer of parents' willingness to lie for their children.

When my youngest son was in eighth grade, we attended the science fair to see all the projects children allegedly built. I compelled my son to create his own project from basement items. His idea was not a technological wonder, but it was unique and it was his own creation. It was an obvious eighth-grade invention.

As we walked through the maze of science projects, I saw an incredible project that would have required a master's degree in engineering. As the boy's father, (who had a master's degree in engineering) explained how the project worked, his son appeared indifferent, even though he'd been awarded first prize. This father and son were presenting an obvious lie and they received an award for it.

Of course, there are more serious issues that parents can lie about for their children. A school board was about to kick a teenager off the team because he was caught drinking alcohol, which is against school policy. Although he was guilty, his mother lied for him. She told school officials that he was home the night he was accused of drinking. They accepted her lie and he stayed on the football team.

I later counseled the mother of the football player. She realized she had told a lie that had many consequences, including harm to her son's character, their relationship, and his view of the world. She realized she granted him permission to lie about any problems in life, with her as his accomplice.

Since she created a relationship with her son founded on distrust and dishonesty, she hindered her son's desire for truth and honesty. When distrust and dishonesty hold a relationship together, eventually the people involved have to ask themselves, "I wonder if he or she would lie to me too?" When this thought surfaces, their relationship will weaken, never allowing trust to grow. Their shared lie will change her son's view of the world. Instead of viewing the world as a place to create trusting relationships, he will view the world as a chess game and view people as pawns that he can manipulate with dishonesty and deceit.

Too Trusting: Overindulgent parents are too trusting.

Some parents, who have dishonest children, are too gullible. Parents want to trust their children, but when children lie they are untrustworthy. Children who lie often defend themselves by saying to their parents, "You should trust me!" This leads overindulgent parents to feel guilty for not trusting their children. They believe that if they were good parents, they should trust their children once again.

In counseling, many overindulgent parents say to me, "I know I should not have trusted my child, but I felt I should give my child one more chance." Because of this thought, their children continually get "one more chance." Overindulgent parents are intelligent people, who know they should not trust their children, but they ignore their good judgment.

A Mentoring Parent's Management of Children's Lying Behavior

Once you discover which of the overindulgent parenting beliefs you use, replace these distorted thoughts by reviewing the qualities of the mentoring parent.

Consider the following ideas and suggestions:

Mentoring parents have a **strong commitment to the truth.** It is important for children to learn that they cannot manipulate their parents with lies and deceit.

Remember the story I told about my father asking me 100 questions to get the truth? I answered every question, but I answered dishonestly— and I was good at it. When he finished asking me questions, he seemed convinced that I was telling the truth. One week later, my father asked me the same one hundred questions. I struggled to recall all the original detailed lies that I said before, but I could not remember. My story was so inconsistent it was obvious that I was lying. My father thoughtfully said to me, "A liar always forgets." He also said to me, "You're a liar" and then he disciplined me. He instilled truth and honesty deep into my soul that day.

There is no substitute for **truth and honesty.** There are no substitutes for truthful labels. When my father said, "You're a liar," I felt shame and humiliation. When attached to good thinking, shame and humiliation are the emotional stings that can motivate positive change. Because of this experience, my desire to avoid the emotional sting of shame and humiliation causes me to be honest. Through this experience I have also learned that an honest life is a less complicated life.

Honesty is a basic value that helps create good self-esteem, character, and relationships. When children exaggerate to gain your attention, it is helpful to **consider the amount and quality of time you spend with your children.** Exaggeration suggests a child has unmet needs for attention. Be open to self-appraisal and decide if you need to make changes with the time you spend with your children.

To reduce gullibility and susceptibility to guilt trips, **trust your emotions and take time to think—contemplate.** Indignation is an appropriate reaction when children try to manipulate you with guilt. When children use guilt to manipulate you, they are insulting you. They are suggesting that you are dumb enough to fall for their manipulative guilt trips. That is not the case, of course, but parents need to be aware of their children's shenanigans. So, don't get guilty, get indignant.

> *When Diana realized her daughter was trying to manipulate her, she became indignant, saying in a very rational tone, "You are trying to manipulate me with a guilt trip. It will not work. If you want something from me, you better be straightforward and honest. Then I will tell you how you can earn what you want. Guilt trips won't work."*

Stealing

The Purpose of Stealing:

Young children occasionally take something that does not belong to them. Children may take a candy-bar from a grocery store, steal money from their parents, or heist a cherished toy from a sibling's bedroom. Most parents employ the traditional discipline of having their children apologize and make restitution.

As with persistent lying, persistent stealing in the form of shoplifting is both a serious psychological and legal issue. Manipulative lying usually accompanies children's stealing because they need to cover their tracks.

Over   What is interesting about shoplifting is that most children, who shoplift, have access to money. They could easily buy the merchandise they are stealing. Most shoplifting children also know right from wrong. So why do children shoplift?

Listed below are several common reasons:

1. The most common reason children shoplift is for the rush of excitement.
2. Some children shoplift to make their parents angry.
3. Other children shoplift to call attention to issues they find disturbing within their family.
4. Many children feel entitled and justified when stealing, because they believe they should be able to take whatever they want. These children have a greater commitment to stealing. They often enter the legal system because their stealing is persistent. When caught, most children blame their friends for the shoplifting and claim they just happened to be there. This excuse is usually a familiar lie. These children usually intended to

steal. Parents need to hold shoplifting children accountable. If they don't, they may be using one of the following overindulgent parenting beliefs:

Overindulgent Parenting Beliefs That Encourage Stealing:

Shield from Consequences: Overindulgent parents shield their children from the consequences of their children's actions, as well as the complications of life.

When parents pamper their children, their children expect special privileges. When police arrest overindulged children who shoplift, these children expect special privileges from the storeowner and police. When children do not receive special privileges from "others," they become angry, not at themselves, but at authority figures.

Overindulged children, who steal, pick their own "points of responsibility." For example, when an overindulged boy misbehaves at school and is disciplined, he does not focus on his misbehavior. Instead, he picks another "point of responsibility." He believes the school officials are the problem, since they are overreacting. He believes the school officials are unfair. It is always someone else's fault.

The same is true for shoplifting children. Many shoplifting children do not believe the problem started with their decision to shoplift. Shoplifting children pick another "point of responsibility". They blame the storeowner for being a jerk because the storeowner overreacted by calling the police. If the children's parents agree with them, they shield their children from appropriate consequences. This leads children to believe that others are unjustly punishing them, and consequently, they learn nothing about changing their misbehavior.

Here is another complication. Overindulgent parents falsely inflate children's egos; so overindulged children believe they are more capable than they actually are. Most children who shoplift believe they are much smarter than adults. They believe they can outsmart anyone, so when police arrest them imagine their surprise.

A Mentoring Parent's Management of Children's Stealing Behavior:

One rule of thumb is that once children steal, it is easier for them to steal again. Another rule of thumb states that if police arrest children for stealing, especially shoplifting, it is rarely their first theft.

Mentoring parents always have children confess, apologize, make restitution, and accept consequences when they steal. When children's stealing includes shoplifting, mentoring parents get counseling for their children. It is especially important that parents **do not buffer** their children from the legal **consequences** of shoplifting.

Summary

Much of children's misbehavior is temporary. But misbehavior has the potential to become permanent and damage parent-child relationships. We cannot always control our children's behavior. We do have control of how we choose to react to our children when they misbehave. Always check your reactions to your children's misbehavior to check if your reactions reflect any of the overindulgent parenting principles. Then correct your reactions by reviewing and using the qualities of the mentoring parent.

In Chapter 5, you will receive many parenting tools that sharpen mentoring skills.

~ CHAPTER 5 ~

The "Tool Box" for the Mentoring Parent

Changing from overindulgence to mentoring requires parenting tools to build better mentoring relationships with children. This chapter gives you the tools you need to become a mentoring parent. Use the tools you feel most comfortable with, but also stretch and use tools that may be new and unusual. Also, consider using a combination of these parenting tools.

Children are so unique that one parenting tool may work well for one of your children, but the same tool may be completely ineffective for your other children. Mix these tools as creatively as you can. It is also helpful to discuss and rehearse these parenting ideas with your spouse.

Consider the parenting tools in this "Toolbox". They will give you the practical skills you need to become a mentoring parent.

Assessing Family Safety

We are starting with family safety first. Children will not make behavioral changes if they do not feel safe. It is vital for families to have a feeling of safety. To consider the issue of family safety, consider this question: "Does your family feel safe?"

One way to help you determine the safe feeling within your family is to consider how you feel as you approach your home. As you enter your home do you feel tension or apprehension? If not, great! If so, realize it is more difficult for children because their tender skills do not manage tension well.

Continually review and use the qualities of the mentoring parent. These qualities promote a safe and encouraging family atmosphere. You can further assess your family's safe feelings by considering these questions:

 ⬥ Is it safe and comfortable to discuss any issue in your family?
 ⬥ Are you and your spouse united and bonded on most family issues, especially with managing your children?
 ⬥ Does your family routinely and freely talk throughout the week?
 ⬥ Is there a balance in your family relationships? In other words, is there one-on-one time with each child? Does your family do activities together? Are there spouse-only times?
 ⬥ Do you give equal love for your children, but parent your children differently?

If you answered "yes" to most of these questions, then your family feels safe. If your answers are mostly "no," start using the qualities of the mentoring parent and the tools throughout this chapter.

Discipline by Design

Too often, discipline happens impulsively or not at all. Discipline needs planning and well-defined goals. Parents who plan discipline together gain a greater bond and become more effective. Listed below is a good working foundation for discipline that I often suggest to parents.

1. When your children misbehave, forewarn them that discipline will occur if they continue. Don't threaten them. Just make a no-nonsense factual statement.
2. Tell your children the exact misbehaviors they need to change before disciplining them. This alone may stop some of your children's misbehavior.
3. If the forewarning does not work, use discipline. I cannot advise you which discipline is the best all-purpose discipline. Each child is so unique that a discipline that is effective for one child may be ineffective for another child. My best suggestions are time-out, loss of special activities, temporary increase of chores, and extra homework.
4. After you discipline, tell your children exactly what they need to do differently and how they can make amends. Children need to change their misbehavior, but they also need a chance to redeem themselves, so offer exact instructions to your children on what they can do to make amends.

Consider the following example of a parent using a healthy foundation of discipline.

A dad instructed his ten-year-old son, who had terrible handwriting, to rewrite his homework. Although the boy promised his dad that he would do it, his father forewarned him that he would discipline him if

*he did not correct his homework. When the father
later asked if the homework was complete, the boy
assured him it was done.*

*When his father asked to see it, the boy hedged. It
became obvious to the father that his son did not complete the homework. Finally the boy reluctantly
offered his original homework.*

*The father quickly realized that he was looking at
the original homework. He told his son that he had
committed two wrongs. First, he lied about his homework and lying was unacceptable. Second, he did not
rewrite his homework.*

*The father was consistent with his forewarning and
disciplined the boy. After the discipline, the father
clearly told the boy that he still needed to complete
the work and to not lie about it.*

This boy felt guilty that he lied to his father, but his
guilt was "good guilt", as he was lying. "Good guilt" creates self-guidance, which encourages children to correct
their behavior in the future. This young man's self-guidance
will now say to him, "In order not to feel bad about lying, I
need to do my work and tell the truth." He also felt disappointed in himself. But his disappointment passed when he
completed the work, which made him feel better. His father
quickly praised his son's finished work.

This father had a firm parenting-framework. He did not
grope for ideas on how to discipline his son. His parenting
framework gave his son predictable guidance without a
frustrated and ineffective parent. Also, this parent did not let
his son off the hook. He taught him to be responsible.

Consider his parenting framework based on the qualities of the mentoring parent:

- He made his son face the **truth** that the schoolwork needed correction.
- He **advised** his son on exactly what he needed to do – rewrite the homework.
- He **monitored** his son to insure the homework was complete.
- He truthfully told his son **reality** (he did not edit)—that he was lying and did not complete the work.
- He **disciplined** his son.
- He **instructed** his son on exactly what to do to correct the situation (quit lying and get the work done).
- He **monitored** his son again and **praised** him when the work was finished.

This is a parent who is not concerned about being a buddy. This parent is mentoring!

Compare the above example with the example below of an ineffective discipline:

Before this same father built his mentoring foundation, he did not parent well. His boy was reluctant to dress up to go to dinner at a fancy restaurant, and was raising a fuss. "Okay, fine," said this frustrated father, "You can go to your grandmother's house while we go out to dinner." The father gave-in to his son's demands and his boy was much happier.

On the way to his grandmother's house, his parents picked up their boy's favorite uncle, who was joining them for dinner. The boy did not realize his favorite uncle was going to dinner too. When they pulled their car into his grandmother's driveway, a boy refused to leave the car, because he wanted to go out to dinner with his favorite uncle. This father

*became frustrated, pulled the boy out of the car, and
spanked him hard, put him in his grandmother's house
and left, never saying one word.*

In this case, this boy did not feel the "good guilt" that
could guide his behavior. He felt intense anger. His father
offered no quality communication, before or after the discipline. Instead, his father reacted with frustration and created
an angry son who felt no compulsion to correct his behavior. His son felt justified in his anger.

If you offer your children a parenting foundation (such
as the discipline guidelines mentioned above), you can
instill a different attitude and motivation in your children.

Forewarning

Forewarning, briefly mentioned above, is such an
important parenting tool it needs more discussion. Very few
overindulgent parents forewarn and follow through with
discipline. So, calmly and firmly offer forewarnings. It is
important that you give only one forewarning, because it is
easy for overindulgent parents to give too many forewarnings,
which reduces its effectiveness. By the way, children do not
usually show that they appreciate a forewarning, but they do.

Paying Money for Discipline

*When my children were small (four and five years
old), they enjoyed sharing the same bedroom together.
There are many advantages to young children having
the same bedroom, but there is also one major disadvantage. They have difficulty falling asleep. In fact,
they get rowdy.*

I found this frustrating as I sat in the living room and listened to their thumping footsteps upstairs, well past their bedtime. Discipline did not help. They just kept thumping.

An idea popped into my head. We went shopping and I bought them wallets. They were ecstatic with their new wallets; all made with neat leather and super-hero emblems. I told them I was going to give them an allowance and they hit the ceiling with happiness. They had a wallet and they had money—$2 every week.

At bedtime that evening, I could hear their usual thumping. When I went upstairs, I forewarned them:

"When Dad is at work, he helps fix children's behavior and they pay him for this help. So, every time I come up here and tell you to stay in bed and go to sleep, you will each have to pay me $1." They were standing on their beds and looked at each other and blinked. They looked at me with an expression resembling, "Yeah, right!" I went down-stairs and in less than two minutes I heard that familiar thumping noise. I went upstairs and said, "I am here to fix your behavior by telling you to go to bed. That will be one dollar." They went to their wallets and each gave me one dollar. I eventually earned enough money to buy lunch and I never heard any thumping noise again.

Younger children respond well to this technique. It is so important that children earn their allowance. Unfortunately, this is not happening in most families today. Many parents are being "five-dollared" into financial straits by children calling parents cheap as they complain, "It's only five dollars!" Children need to earn their money and they need to pay for their discipline. When they do not earn their money, they learn to ask for money and they do nothing to earn it. Imagine asking your boss for extra money and offering nothing in return. The world does not work that way and neither should parenting.

A "Problem-Solving" Attitude

When something goes wrong in life, a healthy question for parents to ask is, "What are my choices to correct this situation?" This is the cornerstone of success in life, and especially for successful parenting. Children need to see their parents' problem-solving attitude, especially when they are on the receiving end of advice or discipline.

Children gain this problem-solving attitude when parents guide and discipline them. Imagine your child has a bully bothering him or her:

Problem-Solving Issue # 1: You can help your child gather all the relevant facts. Where does this occur? Who knows about it? What does the bully want?

Problem-Solving # 2: Offer insights by explaining why someone chooses to be a bully. Tell your children that bullies need to feel "bully power" because they do not have real empowerment in their life.

Problem-Solving # 3: Help your child assess all the possible choices. If the bully hangs out in one area, advise your child to stay away from that area, tell a teacher or try to stay with a group.

Problem-Solving # 4: Allow your child to pick one of the choices. It is tempting to lead your child toward a particular choice, but it is important your child make the choice. Making choices is an important life-sustaining skill.

Problem-Solving # 5: Allow your child to live with the decision for some time, then help the child to evaluate if the choice is working. Does it need changing? Does a different choice need consideration?

As you teach this "problem-solving" attitude to your children, youngsters can eventually use these skills when you are not around. This helps children gain self-guidance, self-reliance and self-confidence.

Self-Appraisal

Many parents do a wonderful job encouraging and praising their children. Encouragement is positive statements parents use to keep children motivated toward self-improvement. Praise is the tribute children receive once they arrive at the improvement. Mentoring parents praise children with love, affection, and status. They do not give toys and activities, as praise is their bond with their children.

Another helpful tool parents can give their children to increase self-reliance and self-esteem is self-appraisal. For example:

A boy came home with a good report card and gave it to his mother. Mom, who encourages the boy with his studies, exclaims, "That's great!" (Praise). To create self-appraisal and increase self-reliance, his mom may ask, "How do you feel about your grades?" This helps the boy create an independent self-appraisal.

171

Sometimes self-appraisal may feel bad because children have negative qualities or may experience failure. One goal as parents is to train children to cope with these difficult times without self-criticism. In gradual steps, encourage your children with honest appraisals of their progress. Ask them how they feel about their progress. If you do, you are helping your children feel the emotional change that comes with good behavior change.

For example, a good boss can correct an employee with honey (care and sincerity), while pointing-out flaws that need correction. As the corrections occur, the good boss continues to praise the employee, and the employee feels better. A lousy boss uses vinegar (condemns and criticizes) to correct an employee, which increases the employee's anger, frustration, and opposition. By offering care, sincerity, encouragement, praise, and honest appraisal to your children, you can guide them to appraise their own progress.

Not-So-Natural Consequences

There is notable discussion in this book, and many others, about allowing children to endure the natural consequences of their misbehavior. Natural consequences are consequences that occur naturally in a situation. For example, if a girl does not study for a test, she naturally fails. If a teenage boy does not maintain his car, the car naturally falls apart. These are natural consequences.

On the other hand, "not-so-natural" consequences are by parental design. "Not-so-natural" consequences have a great advantage over natural consequences because parents can safely use them without the inconvenience of natural consequences. For example:

Nancy habitually parked her car in the street on snowy nights. Her parents forewarned her the city will tow her car away if the snowplows come through during the night. I suggested to her parents a "not-so-natural" consequence.

Instead of allowing the natural consequences of the city towing her car away, her parents parked her car in their garage. In the morning, Nancy was worried because her car was gone, until her parents told her it was in the garage. She experienced the emotional sting of her car being towed, without having to experience the actual event. You would think Nancy learned a valuable lesson. Believe it or not, it did not help.

The next snowy evening, Nancy left her car parked in the street again. In spite of her parents' insistence, she left it there. That night, her parents put her car in the garage to prevent the city from towing her car away. The next morning Nancy saw her car was missing. She strolled directly to the garage to get her car, but she could not find her car keys. Her mother told Nancy that to get her keys, Nancy would have to pay a $35 towing fee.

The next snowy night, Nancy parked her car in the driveway. Nancy's parents created "not-so-natural" consequences, so Nancy experienced the consequence of losing her car and paying a fee. But, with no inconvenience to her parents.

Notice the learning experience was not effective until Nancy paid a $35 fine to her parents. It is very helpful to blend various parenting tools together. Nancy's discipline included "not-so-natural consequences" and paying for her discipline.

"Not-so-natural consequences" is one of my favorite parenting tools. You can become very creative with this tool. Here are several more examples where "not-so-natural consequences" had a good impact:

Glenda is fifteen-years-old and shares a bathroom with her parents. Every morning when her dad finally gets access to the bathroom, Glenda's makeup, hair dryer, curling iron, deodorant, and shampoo are disarrayed throughout the bathroom. Nothing is in its place!

I advised her dad to forewarn his daughter that he would confiscate her bathroom "stuff" the next time it was left out. She would not get it back! She tested his warning and lost all of her grooming supplies.

When she failed to keep her things in order, her stuff was gone—history! The result is a fifteen-year-old girl facing school without her make-up, cologne, deodorant, hair spray, and shampoo. It was important that she replace her supplies with her own money. Eventually, Glenda realized that to keep her "stuff," she needed to put it away.

Since clothes and toys are too expensive to throw away, I advise parents to lock them up when using this confiscation technique. Parents can gradually give clothes and toys back, as their children's cleanliness improves.

⚬⫘⚬

Another example involves Alex, a bright boy who refused to work hard at school and had the uncanny ability to make his homework his parents' problem. Although he never worried about his near-failing grades, his parents did. Despite their best efforts, Alex refused to do his homework.

Often when counseling this issue, I suggest a two-step technique.

***Step 1:** I recommend that parents forewarn their children about natural consequences. For example, when an intellectually bright child like Alex refuses to work and his parents offer every form of help, I forewarn him about the future. "When you are 18 and graduating (we hope) from high school, your parents will be free to do whatever they want. They'll have more money, might retire, who knows." This leaves the impression that Alex's grades will have no affect on the quality of his parents' lives. I continue, "At age 18, what you did or did not do in high school is your problem. You will have to explain to a potential employer why you have a 1.4 grade point average." Alex said, "I don't care," but he still got the message.*

***Step 2:** I also tell parents this problem is an ownership issue. Is it their problem or Alex's problem that he refuses to study? It is Alex's problem. Next, I advised Alex's parents to do something that is difficult for invested parents to do: to let go of ownership of Alex's education. No more nagging about homework or assignments. No pressure to achieve. I told his parents that this problem belongs to Alex.*

When his parents gave up ownership, Alex had to decide if he would accept ownership of his schoolwork or not. He lost the power of pushing his parents' educational button in order to frustrate and worry them. I directed Alex's parents to focus on retirement plans. I suggested they should invest his college fund into their retirement fund. Studying is now Alex's problem. Going to college is now Alex's problem.

Many children intentionally get low grades to push their parents' buttons. The above two-step strategy erases parents' reactions when their educational buttons are pushed. Often parents find themselves in a never-ending cycle of their children's sabotage. Since parents are continuously telling their children how important grades are, their children use this information to anger their parents. The more parents try, the less children work.

Instead, parents can use the two-step process of forewarning, and give back ownership (and all its consequences) to underachieving children. I understand this is difficult for parents. I remind parents that many people who were successful in life performed poorly in high school.

If parents suggest that life is over because of children's poor high school performance, children believe it. Everyone grows at different rates physically, academically, emotionally, cognitively, socially, and spiritually. I tell parents to remember their high school reunion and consider the people they never expected to do well, but did.

As an aside, I do not believe in paying for children's college. College offers two types of education: a special field of study that students are interested in pursuing, and a money management degree. As college students pay for their own college, they learn resourcefulness when times are tight, as well as money management. Overindulged children do not gain this second education, which is as important as a field of study. College students have many choices in paying for their college today. Ask any college guidance counselor if you want more information. Better yet, have your college-bound child make the inquiry.

Get rid of the fear that poor high school achievement will damage your children's future. When children decide it is time to succeed, they will. Like everyone else, they will have to pay their dues. That is a natural consequence.

Refinement

Think back to the previous example of Nancy's car being towed. It illustrates another parenting tool—refinement. The first time Nancy's parents put her car in the garage, their strategy did not work. Nancy still parked her car on the street during snowy nights. Her parents did not give up complaining, "This stuff does not work!" Instead, they refined their discipline by adding another tool (making Nancy pay for her discipline).

One of the greatest parenting flaws is that many parents try a new parenting tool once and then give up in frustration, because the tool did not work. Some parents say, "We tried everything and nothing works with this child." On a rare occasion, this may be true.

What I usually see is parents drifting from one parenting tool to another without refining their parenting tools. Refinement is essential for parenting, especially for parents of young children because they are more likely to model their parents. If their parents are adapting by refining their parenting tools, children also learn to adapt and to refine.

There are several ways to refine discipline. They include:

1. Realize the same discipline may not work for all children, because of the unique features of different children.
2. Blend a combination of several parenting tools to create more effective discipline.
3. Don't believe it when your children seem unaffected by discipline! Children often pretend discipline does not bother them. Continue to be persistent with your planned discipline and gauge your success, not by your children's pretense of not being bothered, but by keeping your parenting plan in place.

When children pretend a discipline does not bother them, parents often give-up in frustration, which reinforces children's disobedience. Be persistent with your parenting plan! Remember, you can only control your actions, not your children's actions.

Classify Behavior

To help decide the severity of children's misbehavior, plus your course of action, it is helpful to learn to classify children's behavior. Here are practical classifications:

Good behavior leads children to receive rewards and creates positive self-guidance.

A *behavioral concern* is a misbehavior that is not particularly harmful to the child or others.

An *alarming behavior* is misbehavior that has the potential to emotionally or physically hurt someone. An "alarming behavior" is obvious and persistent. Parents need a parenting plan to help their children eradicate alarming behavior.

An *extreme behavior* is a misbehavior that is hurting someone and needs immediate attention, a parenting plan, and counseling. A pattern of extreme behavior suggests conduct disorder.

These classifications are helpful to determine if you should simply ignore your children's misbehavior, create a parenting plan based on the principles of this book, or initiate counseling.

Discipline Without an Audience

The goal of discipline does not include embarrassment or humiliation of children. On the contrary, it means teaching children to learn, bond, and experience the consequences of making decisions, both good and bad. It is not always possible, but usually best if you discipline children in private. This lessens their embarrassment and humiliation.

Here are two notable exceptions to this rule:

1. There are times when it is necessary to discipline children in front of their friends, especially if their misbehavior is extreme and harmful. The priority of removing the potential harm to others may override the concern for the child's personal embarrassment.

2. Some children have poor self-guidance, because their overindulgent parents protect them from natural embarrassment and humiliation. They never learned the impact of their behavior on others. Public discipline, that includes feedback from children they hurt, may help them understand their impact on others.

Children, like adults, need to be humble, but excessive and distorted embarrassment and humiliation can erode self-esteem. Usually, discipline offered privately is best.

Again, there needs to be special circumstances to discipline children in front of others, as mentioned above. It is best to offer a forewarning first. If you forewarn your children, then discipline your children in public if the misbehavior continues, the next time you forewarn your children, they usually become more responsive.

Ignoring Children's Behavior

Ignoring children's behavior is a highly overrated parenting tool. It can be appropriate with minor misbehavior in young children, if their behavior is annoying and attention-getting. Often children are getting too much attention from other children when they misbehave, so this tool becomes ineffective.

Coaching, Rehearsal, and Choices

I am going to tell you a secret that I never share with any children, but will share with you. When it comes to children, parents have no power! Parents have power when their children are young, but power fades quickly as children become teenagers.

Teenagers need their parents' influence. That is why your sound advice and predictions for your children are so important. When your children have confidence in the consistency of your advice and predictions, you gain more influence as your children mature.

Coach, rehearse, and give children the gradual power to make their own choices. This is incredibly important because today's children have many sources for bad advice. They also have more disturbing role models for misbehavior than ever before. In other words, today's parents have more competition than parents of previous generations—competition that influences children's beliefs, and competition which often runs counter to parents' beliefs. An excellent antidote is to combine coaching, rehearsal, and choice.

Coaching

Coaching occurs when you teach your children to manage life. It is vital that your style of coaching changes as your children become teenagers and adults. For purposes of safety, parents need to be over-controlling when their children are toddlers because of toddlers' inability to understand what may harm them. For example, toddlers do not realize that a wall socket could shock them. So, parents need to over-control their children until they are old enough to realize the dangerous issues of life.

For the first several years, parents' over-control of their children protects their children. As children grow, your coaching style needs to change. The goal for parents, as children turn into adults, is to be less controlling and to become more influential. You can accomplish this by using the qualities of the mentoring parent and the parenting tools provided in this chapter.

Each child grows at a different rate, so it is difficult to tell you exactly when you need to become more "influential" and less "controlling." Some parents never make the transition from control talk to coaching.

We discussed an earlier example where I counseled a mother (Ruth) who talked to her married daughter as if her daughter was a toddler. This mother was constantly giving advice as if her daughter was a child. She used her money to make her daughter bend to her wishes, because her daughter was financially dependent. She controlled many parts of her daughter's marital relationship and childrearing. When I counseled her about her need to control her daughter, she realized she never made the transition from control talk to coaching. She also realized that she never created her own identity. She was trying to live her life through her daughter. She relinquished her control talk and became more influential with her daughter.

Rehearsal

Children benefit from rehearsal. Rehearsal is one of the best methods for changing children's behavior. Parents often tell children what not to do when they misbehave. When parents tell their children how to improve their behavior, children may not fully understand.

When adults receive verbal instruction, they have abstract reasoning, so they can easily imagine the actual changes they need to make. Children, on the other hand, have a harder time imagining these changes. They need to actually experience replacement behaviors.

With rehearsal, you can help your children practice the exact behaviors they need to use. Your children can experiment with various behaviors to help decide which options are best. Rehearsal allows children to be comfortable with new choices before they actually try them at home, in school, and on the playground.

Rehearsal is natural for children because it is exactly like play. For example, parents of the 1950's had more time to parent. Back then homes had screen doors that closed with a tight spring. These doors would bang like a shotgun when children let go of them. Slamming doors irritated 1950's parents. They did not say, "Don't slam the door!" Instead, they instructed their children to go outside, walk through the door again, and quietly close the door. Rehearsals! Teachers also use rehearsal with children. When children run in a hallway, teachers instruct the "sprinters" to back up and walk the entire distance again. This is rehearsal.

Use rehearsal for all types of behavior problems. It is especially helpful when children are in difficult situations and you cannot be there to help. For example:

> *When visiting her uncle, eight-year-old Jackie's uncle would often ask her gossip-type questions. He would isolate and interrogate her. She felt trapped and uncomfortable, because he was so big and she was so small.*
>
> *Just before their next visit to her uncle's home, Jackie mentioned this problem with her mother. I suggested that we rehearse several scenarios for her that she could use when her uncle asked his meddlesome questions.*

On her next visit, her uncle employed his usual tactics, and started to ask intrusive gossip-type questions about her family. Jackie took her uncle by the hand and said, "Come with me." He followed her into the living room, where her parents were sitting. Just like she rehearsed she announced, "He is asking me all those stupid questions again." Then she looked at him and said, "You can ask my parents those stupid questions."

Her rehearsed solution was empowering. It helped her gain the support of her parents and the freedom to play with her cousins—without her uncle's harassment.

Another easy solution would be to have one of her parents talk to the uncle. But, that solution would not offer several important lessons:

♒

Jackie learned that her mentoring parents offer real solutions, so when difficult times occur, Jackie is more likely to go to her parents for guidance. Jackie realized that her parents help her feel empowered. This is vital in parenting! If she knows she can go to her mentoring parents for real solutions, she feels more protected.

Jackie also gained a new skill, the power of rehearsal. When she rehearses for other issues, she can plan her actions before she proceeds. When young children rehearse solutions with their parents, they eventually mentally rehearse choices before taking an action.

Rehearsal empowers children. It also bonds children with their mentoring parents. Rehearsing choices with children gives them the opportunity to practice and gain more confidence to manage difficult situations.

There are times when you cannot directly help your children correct a problem. But you can design opportunities for your children to rehearse sticky situations. To cite a specific example:

Mitch's father saw few social skills in his 14-year-old son. His son was lonely, and ate lunch every day alone in the high school cafeteria. In fact, he did everything alone. This father did not know how to teach his son to socialize with other children. So he contacted the school's peer program that helps children with various problems. The coordinating school counselor of the school's peer program was glad to help.

When Mitch went to the cafeteria to eat alone, a student sat with him and casually talked to him. Then another student sat next to him and talked to him too. He got his first invitation to a football game. Several months later, the school peer program members invited him to become a peer counselor.

This mentoring father realized that if children interacted with his son, his son could model their social skills. All he had to do was discover how to expose his son to social children. Because he found a way to make this happen, Mitch never ate alone again. He developed many friendships. That's a mentoring parent!

Choice

The more choices children have for solutions, the better. I usually like to rehearse more than one choice when children have any problem, so they have many possible solutions. If one choice does not work, you can encourage your children to try the next choice.

Rules About Rules

There are "rules about rules" that our children need to learn. For example, mentoring parents advocate that children should not fight, but they do not want their children beaten without defending themselves. The rule is "do not fight," but children need to know the exceptions to the rules. This is often a problem for children when there are situations with conflicting values. They are uncertain which values they should prioritize.

For example, if a child sees a friend do something illegal, such as steal from a store, the child may have difficulty deciding which value is a greater priority. Should the value of loyalty to friends take precedence over the value of not keeping secrets from parents? Mentoring parents prepare children by discussing examples of these moral dilemmas long before moral crises occur. Parents can teach their children the "rules about rules."

In the example of loyalty to friends versus keeping secrets from parents, the "rules about rules" dilemma depends on which value has a greater priority for the parents.

If parents believe that loyalty to friends is the most important priority, then parents should teach their children when loyalty to friends becomes illegal behavior. If parents believe the most important priority is not keeping secrets from parents, then parents would teach their children how to keep confidentiality, and how to make appropriate exceptions.

Unfortunately, teaching children "rules about rules" rarely happens until a problem occurs, when knowing the "rules about rules" would have been helpful. Mentoring parents can rehearse with their children the "rules about rules" philosophy and offer children possible solutions for future moral dilemmas.

Rehearsal is a good technique, but there is no guarantee that children will choose rehearsed solutions. Even though children may not use the rehearsed solutions when a moral problem occurs, they eventually realize the rehearsed solutions would have produced a better outcome. This realization will help shape their decisions in the future.

Compliment Good Behavior

Complimenting good behavior is a technique that works well for younger children, especially with their shorter attention span. Kindergarten teachers are experts with this tool. When kindergarten teachers mention that one child is behaving well, the other children start behaving with the hope of getting their teacher's compliment.

Younger children automatically respect their teacher, but this is not always true of older children. If a high school teacher compliments a child's behavior during class, other children may ridicule the complimented child.

However, children of all ages need compliments. With younger children, parents can give compliments to change children's behavior. With older children, parents should give compliments without attempting to change their behavior. Older children need honest compliments that offer encouragement.

So for younger children, use compliments to encourage your children to change their behavior. I encourage you to eliminate agendas when using compliments on older children, and praise them purely for the sake of complimenting.

"Thinking–Feeling" Questions and Making Amends

One mentoring tool, that increases parents' influence to help their children understand their impact on others, is to ask children "thinking and feeling" questions. For example:

> "How do you think Grandmother felt when you gave her flowers?"
> "What do you think it feels like to be punched the way you punched your brother?"
> "How did you feel when you gave money to that charity?"
> "How would you feel if someone stole your favorite toy?"

Mentoring parents ask children "thinking-feeling" questions to motivate them to think about how they effect others. One mother saw her son intentionally break his friend's favorite toy. This mentoring mother asked her son a "thinking-feeling" question so he would understand how his actions affected his friend, "How do you think it feels to have your toy broken?" To make amends, she also instructed him to give his favorite toy to his friend. "Thinking and feeling" questions teach children to think twice before they act. "Thinking and feeling" questions also promote empathy for others.

Through "thinking and feeling" questions, children learn that making amends will heal relationships and helps children realize we are all connected.

Align Children's Feelings and Thoughts

Because children are just beginning to learn about their emotions, they often confuse emotional words. When a boy says, "I hate my sister!" parents often respond, "No, you don't!" But for that moment, this boy is actually angry with his sister. Minutes later, the same children are often playing together. Children have difficulty distinguishing between different emotions. When this boy is calmer, he needs to be mentored to use correct words such as, "I am angry with my sister."

When teaching children about the abstract words of emotions, I have found that a children's dictionary is helpful. A dictionary gives parents a simple way to express abstract words to children. Teach your children the accurate meaning for the words of emotions.

Eliminate Judgmental Talk But Keep Your Judgment!

Have you ever screamed at any of your children, "What is wrong with you?" This is a tough question for children to hear. Their answers can be even tougher. This question, "What is wrong with you?" is actually a broad-brush statement which leads children to believe they have so many flaws that they are defective.

Being judgmental occurs when parents distort their children's understanding of themselves. Judgmental talk requires the use of distorted labels. When children are described as bad, they may accept this distorted label. Since judgmental talk is distorting children's view of themselves, remove distorted judgmental talk.

Judgmental talk does not include conversations when parents are honestly pointing out children's flaws. It is a mentoring parents job to point out and help correct children's flaws, and at the same time assure children that they can change.

Personal Empowerment

Children need to learn what they can influence and what they cannot influence. This is an idea that mentoring parents need to teach their children. For example, if there is a death, divorce, or other trauma, parents can teach their children what they can and cannot change about the difficult life experience.

I counsel many children who fantasize that if they are good, keep their grades up, help more around the house, then their parents will not divorce or their dead loved one will come back. While it is important for children and parents to express all of their emotions about a traumatic event, we must empower traumatized children with the truth, using as much support and empathy as possible.

Touching Messages of Love

Frequent hugs and caring touch are important for growing children. Parents can create a bond by gently touching a child's shoulder. Most children are comfortable with different forms of physical affection. Mentoring parents can gauge the type of affection with which each of their children is comfortable, and use it.

Younger children may be more comfortable with a big burley hug, while many teenagers seem to be uncomfortable with physical affection from their parents. Parents need to get creative to keep physical affection alive with their teenagers.

One form of affectionate touch, that most mothers hate, is wrestling. I am convinced that father and son wrestling is a teenage form of hugging, but I am having a hard time convincing mothers of this fact! Mothers are typically upset with wrestling dads and teenagers in the living room, but it is a great way for self-conscious teenagers to preserve a touching relationship.

Some children are open to physical affection when their friends are not around. Other children are responsive to a touch on the shoulder or back, while others feel comfortable with a full bear hug. The important point is that you need to preserve physical affection with your children.

Humor

More than any other parenting tool, I have ended many heated family battles in my counseling office with humor. Here are several rules for using humor:

1. Humor should not hurt or put-down others.
2. Humor should not avoid or make light of important issues.
3. Humor should be directed at the situation and not at family members involved in a conflict.
4. Humor should not be overused.
5. Humor is a tool that is acceptable for parents to use with all types of children's misbehavior, except "extreme behavior" that is harmful to others.

When family tension needs decompression, humor and rage are two tools for releasing that tension. I prefer humor, since it is much less abusive than rage. Humor can also strengthen the bond between parents and children that rage can never offer.

One of my favorite examples of humor occurred when a girl tried to push her mother's button to make her angry. Instead of reacting with her predictable temper tantrum, her mother started singing, "The hills are alive with the sound of music..." As she danced through the house the entire family started to sing, leaving her daughter both shocked and perplexed! Her mother was humorously saying, "You will not push my buttons." Instead of angrily confronting her daughter, she turned it into a happy memory.

Humor can create wonderful memories that last a lifetime. Humor is much more effective than intimidation and rage, because it promotes a safe and harmonious family atmosphere.

Humility

"When I'm wrong, I'm wrong." Parents admitting when they are wrong sounds obvious, but the number of parents I have counseled that never admit when they are wrong is astounding. Often these same parents become upset when their children never admit when they are wrong. They wonder, "Where did this child learn to be so stubborn?"

Admitting their mistakes and making apologies keep people humble and willing to accept their own flaws, which is the first step in correcting flaws. In fact, if parents model humility, they create humble and respectful children. When parents refuse to admit to mistakes, their children assume that it is not safe to apologize or make amends. Admitting their mistakes and offering apologies are good tools for building children's character. Humility is an excellent quality for parents to model for their children.

Time-Out

The first time I used time-out, I got the strongest arm muscles I have ever had. I decided that I was going to use a comfortable chair in my bedroom as the time-out chair for my children. It was a boring place with no toys, distractions, or entertainment.

When my youngest son was three, he was "strong-willed," so I created a parenting plan using time-out. When he misbehaved, I placed him in the time-out chair while I calmly explained the behaviors he needed to change. As I left, he followed me out the door and down the hall. During the next hour, I placed him back into that time-out chair over 100 times. He was testing me to the point of fatigue! If I had given up, his misbehavior would have continued.

Finally, he stayed in the time-out chair. Eventually, this bedroom chair became his place to "cool off." He would often go in there on his own accord when he felt tempted to misbehave. He would often stay there 30-to-45 minutes and leave with a positive attitude. Instead of the time-out chair becoming a notorious punishment, it became a tool to help him release pressure. Recently we tried to throw this old chair out, but he wanted us to keep it because it was his childhood "cooling off" chair. It sits in his room today and I suspect now that he is an adult, he will take it with him when he leaves.

Time-out has real advantages because it is neither an intrusive nor a physically painful discipline. Time-out allows children time to think and cool off—or fall asleep. Parents also get a break (when the testing is over) when they use time-out. Time-out's greatest advantage is its potential in becoming a "cooling off" catalyst.

Spanking

I advise parents to not spank—but then there are "rules about rules." Is there ever a time when spanking is acceptable and not damaging to children?

Some parents should never spank their children. This is especially true of abusive parents. For other children, it is an individual decision for parents. Like most issues in life, there are no black and white answers. Most people who say they will never spank children either do not have children, have young children, or they allow their children to become unruly.

I do not agree with the current trend of psychological thought that says all spanking is bad and always damaging to children. I do agree that spanking needs to be part of a parenting plan which stops spanking from becoming abusive. Here are my suggestions, if you feel that spanking is suitable for your children:

1. Spanking is appropriate for strong-willed children who do not respond to other forms of discipline.
2. Spanking should be a final resort; after all other types of discipline have failed.
3. Parents should never spank children when they feel overwhelming frustration.
4. If one parent is not comfortable with spanking, the other parent needs to respect that discomfort and not spank their children. Like any other discipline, parents need to agree before using the discipline of spanking.
5. Parents should always forewarn children before spanking.
6. Parents need to state the exact misbehavior children need to change.
7. After the spanking, parents need to teach their children about the amends children need to do to correct their misbehavior.

8. Parents should offer a mild-to-moderate spanking on children's buttocks and never slap children on the face or head.

Spanking should not be a daily event. If it is, parents need to consider other kinds of discipline or family counseling.

~ Final Thoughts ~

Whether you are a Mom or Dad, parenting is the greatest job in the world. It is a joyful job because the foundation of your relationship with your children is love. But never confuse overindulgence with love. Overindulgence usually leads children to a non-loving relationship with their parents.

In fact, overindulgence creates children who have conditional love for their parents. They only contact their parents when they need something: money, a favor or help getting out of trouble. You and your children deserve much more than conditional love.

Overindulgent parents want to be buddies with their children. Mentoring parents become buddies as their children become adults. Mentoring parents give children structure. Children act like they do not want structure, but they do. Make sure they get it.

Your job is to think like a mentoring parent and then - parent. This includes loving your children, insuring their safety, teaching them about God, disciplining, making them face consequences for their actions and more. It does not include buying, leniency, and offering a soft life with no chores.

Love is your best friend when raising your children. Work is your second best friend. Always remember, when your children want something make them work for it. Give them love, food, safety, a home, affection, affiliation and more. But you never have to give televisions, video games, cars or designer clothes to have a real relationship with your children.

Hope is the wish for change. Taking action is the agent of change. I hope this book is an agent of change for you. I hope and pray that your family will have the close emotional bonds that you and they deserve.

$\sim\!\!*\!\!\sim$

I am going to stop where I started. *Put your pocket book away. Love 'me, don't overindulge 'em!*